FLAK AND FERRETS

Also available from Sentinel Publishing:

MOONLESS NIGHT   B. A. James

NO FLIGHT FROM THE CAGE   Calton Younger

FORCED MARCH TO FREEDOM   Robert Buckham

From the MARCH OF THE ROYAL AIR FORCE

Walter Morison

by Lieutenant John Watton, Colditz, 1944

[Frontispiece]

FLAK AND FERRETS

ONE WAY TO COLDITZ

by

Walter Morison

Illustrated

LONDON
SENTINEL PUBLISHING
1995

Flak and Ferrets by Walter Morison

FIRST PUBLISHED IN GREAT BRITAIN IN 1995
BY SENTINEL PUBLISHING

ISBN (Hardback): 1 874767 09 2
ISBN (Paperback): 1 874767 10 6

Printed in England.

Contents

List of Illustrations

Illustrations in Photogravure

Frontispiece: Walter Morison

Between pages 86 and 87
De Havilland DH 82 Tiger Moth
Hawker Hart in the RAF Museum, Hendon
Westland Lysander
Vickers Wellington from 103 Squadron
Wellington cockpit
A room at Sagan
The 'girls' in *French Without Tears*
Lorne Welch
Air pump designed by Lorne Welch for tunnel 'Harry'
A selection of forged passes

Between pages 150 and 151
'Wanted Men'
Junkers W 34
Gotha 145
Welch and Morison after recapture
Welch and Morison at a later photo-call
'To all Prisoners of War'
Skeleton key fashioned by POWs in Colditz
Martin Francis' scale model of the Colditz Glider
Francis, Best and Goldfinch with model of Colditz Glider
Chess set made in Colditz by George Drew
Box lid for George Drew's chess set

Line Drawings and Facsimiles

About the Author

WALTER McDonald Morison was born in Beckenham, Kent, on 26 November, 1919, the son of a stock jobber, or what would now be called a market maker. He was lucky to be educated at Stowe, a school which unlike many others at the time was, he says, educating boys to live in the second half of the twentieth century. He went on to Trinity College, Cambridge, to read Economics, but after a year the war started and without delay he decided to join the RAF, partly because he could already fly.

After the war he qualified as a Chartered Accountant, becoming in time the Senior Partner of his firm, which later became Morison Stoneham. He says that he was never any good as an accountant, but that he enjoyed the challenge of modernising and developing the firm.

Both before and after the war he was a keen glider pilot, but gave it up when family commitments made it impossible to continue at the forefront of the sport. Instead, he took up sailing, and with his wife Joan has cruised from the Hook of Holland to the south of Brittany, particularly enjoying arriving in foreign ports where the wine is cheap and the *moules mariniéres* are plentiful.

For several years now he has worked as a trustee of a charitable foundation engaged in financing medical research, and has enjoyed the stimulating change to dealing with doctors and scientists rather than with finance.

Preface

FOR a few years after the war you could dine out any day if you happened to have been a prisoner at Colditz. Everyone in those days had lived through the war, but now the ranks are thinning out. Most people were born after 1945, or were very young at the time. Yet recently many people I have met have been anxious to hear first-hand experiences, but have often seemed reluctant to ask, feeling perhaps that it would be an intrusion. There are, of course, hundreds of books which they could read, but because so many focus on the great dramas like the Battle of Britain, the Dam Busters, or D-Day, it is difficult to taste in them the flavour of life, and death, as it was lived by tens of thousands of airmen through those six years. Men who may never have won the DFC, let alone the DSO or the VC, but whose lives, heaven knows, had their share of drama, of humour and of tragedy.

And so I wrote *Flak and Ferrets*. It takes off in 1939 when I applied to join the RAF, and ends in 1945 as I walked sadly away from a life which, despite the trauma and the tedium, was all that I had known as an adult and which I had come to love. Between the two the story unwinds through training, by chance becoming a flying instructor, then a bomber pilot and a prisoner of war. Escaping was the POW's sport *par excellence*, and much of the story surrounds the high drama of a classic, but hitherto unpublished escape from Stalag Luft III known as the 'Delousing Party', which led me and Lorne Welch onto a Luftwaffe airfield and into the cockpit of an aircraft, with our eyes focussed on Sweden—an adventure which sadly ended up instead in Colditz.

Flak and Ferrets draws on notes I wrote in 1945 and on my letters home throughout the war, and so it is almost contemporary in the feelings and ideas which it conveys. I hope you enjoy it.

Walter Morison, 1995.

Acknowledgements

THE author would like to express his thanks to the following:
Lorne Welch, without whom half of this story would never
have happened, and Ann Welch, without whose editing none
of it would have been readable; Jack Best and Bill Goldfinch
for details of the Colditz glider; Mr Martin Francis for
permission to reproduce photographs of his scale model of
the Colditz glider; John Beaumont for details of his escape
from Colditz; George Drew for permission to photograph his
chess set; 'After the Battle' for permission to reproduce
their photograph of the Hawker Hart; Mike Vines of 'Photo
Link' for permission to use his air-to-air photograph of the
DH Tiger Moth; Mr David Bowker for permission to
reproduce Group Captain Dudley Burnside's painting of a
Wellington from 103 Squadron; the Imperial War Museum
for permission to use photographs taken in Stalag Luft III
and an air-to-air photograph of a Lysander; the Public
Record Office for permission to reproduce the documents on
pages 51 and 55; the Ministry of Defence for permission to
publish the extracts from 'TEE EMM' on pages 40-43 and to
reproduce the photograph of the Wellington cockpit; the
BBC for permission to publish the News Bulletin on page 173;
and, finally, to 'The Third and Last Reich' for the extract
from the German 'Criminal Police Gazette' and the notice
'To all Prisoners of War'.

The material from both the Public Record Office and the
Ministry of Defence is Crown Copyright and is reproduced
with the permission of the Controller of Her Majesty's
Stationery Office. The material from the BBC is reproduced
with the permission of the BBC Written Archives Centre.

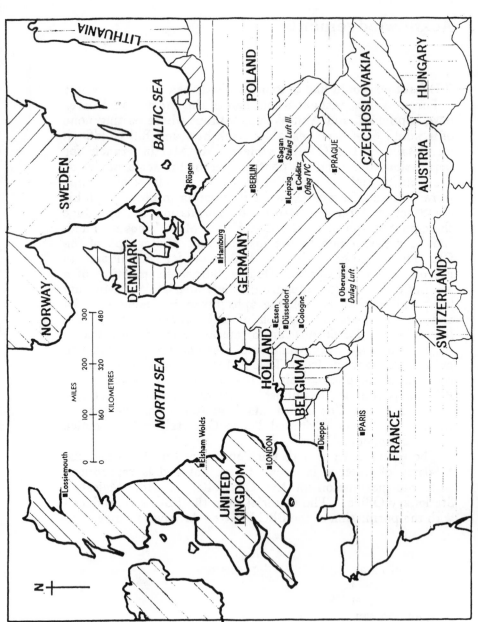

Western Europe showing principal Bomber Command targets and the prisoner-of-war camps in which the author was held.

CHAPTER ONE

War

DEREK Bolton and I stood before the red letter box near my home in Cheam, Surrey, each with a letter to post. We hesitated a moment then, after a quick look at each other, pushed in our envelopes. They fell silently towards the future.

It was 4 September, 1939. Yesterday we had listened on the wireless to Neville Chamberlain telling us that we were at war with Germany, and the almost immediate air raid sirens had sounded the urgency of deciding how to become a part of that war.

Derek and I were both undergraduates at Trinity College, Cambridge, and our letters were applications to join the RAF. Five years later Derek was a Wing Commander, DSO, DFC, commanding a Lancaster squadron, while I had followed a trail which led from flak to ferrets.

In the few hours since the sirens had sounded I had worked through all the possibilities. Why choose the RAF? Why not the Army—or the Navy? Well, not the Army, thank you. The Great War was only twenty years away, and images of the Western Front remained unappealing: mud, trenches, barbed wire, shell fire, thousands mown down by machine guns as they struggled across no-man's land. The Navy then? I knew nothing at all about the sea. How about the Air Force? Ah, yes! I could already fly a glider. In the sky I would be an individual. It would be clean. Aeroplanes were exciting toys. Yes, I would join the Royal Air Force. Was there perhaps a sneaky little voice which said it might be safer? Probably yes, and if so that voice was telling a sick joke.

Our letters were to the Joint Universities Recruiting Board. Very soon I was called for interview, and apprehensively went to Cambridge to present myself, but it was a perfunctory affair. At the end of it the officer said: "Mr Morison, we will recommend you for training as a pilot and for a commission. Of course, this doesn't guarantee either, but all being well you should should get a commission." I was relieved, but I wasn't surprised. That was how it was in those days. Stowe and Trinity. Naturally you became an officer.

But there was still the worrying hurdle of the medical to overcome. Aircrew were required to be a hundred per cent fit, but a couple of years previously I had been seriously ill. Anyway, there was nothing for it but to go before the Medical Officer:

"Deep breath...Breathe out."—Tap, tap.—"Okay."

Blood pressure?—Okay.

Blow up that wretched column of mercury and hold it for a minute.—Okay (well, just).

Eyes.—20/20 vision.—Okay.

The doctor holds your balls.—"Cough please."—Okay.

Why do they always do that? They can't all be queer, or can they?

No, they can't.

So. All okay.

Nothing happened for several long weeks. Then I got orders to report to the RAF barracks at Uxbridge, a great dismal place on the western outskirts of London and totally remote from aeroplanes. I joined the queue of recruits shuffling slowly towards a Flight Sergeant who was checking our names against a list until eventually I stood before him, still every inch a civilian:

"Name?"—"Morison."

"Your number's 903259;"—he looked up—"and get your 'air cut."

"I had it cut yesterday."

"Say that again and I'll knock your fuckin' 'ead off."

Now, abruptly, I was just 903259 Aircraftman Second Class Morison, and you cannot get any lower than that. I was beginning to learn and the first lesson was that when the Flight Sergeant said get your hair cut, you got it cut.

Soon I wandered off to the NAAFI—of vivid memory. It was a vast, hot, smokey cavern, dimly lit, the windows sealed by blackout curtains, and with a great crowd of sweating airmen singing 'South of the Border'. These were erks, the real thing, important people who knew all about looking after aircraft, not raw would-be pilots. 'South of the Border' comes into into my head whenever I remember Uxbridge.

At that early stage of the war the RAF could not cope with training all the people it had recruited so, after being issued with a somewhat prickly uniform, I was sent on indefinite leave. This was the time of the 'Phoney War', when we didn't quite like to shoot at the other side and almost nothing was happening. We had expected immediate devastation of London by the Luftwaffe and even Churchill, writing in *The Second World War*, recalls how as the first sirens sounded: "I gazed from the doorway along the empty street and my imagination drew pictures of ruin and carnage and vast explosions..."; but no bombs were falling, and the RAF was dropping only leaflets.

Although I may now have been the lowest form of animal life in the RAF, I was still an undergraduate at Trinity, so I returned to Cambridge for the autumn term. There I had the advantage of both an RAF uniform and an academic gown (all undergraduates wore gowns in those days), so I was able to play off the RAF police against the university Proctors. Anyway, I was never likely to take another exam and so I could enjoy myself. In Cambridge we knew nothing about the thousands of people being murdered in Poland by the Nazis. There were still punts on the river and in Grantchester "the church clock stood yet at ten to three and there was honey still for tea". It was an innocent and pleasant interlude before the storm.

At the beginning of January 1940 I was, at last, recalled from leave and posted to No.1 Initial Training Wing, which to my delight was also in Cambridge. We were installed in Downing College and whenever possible I continued to enjoy the life of a student. Everyone at the ITW was supposedly training as aircrew of one sort or another, though we who fancied ourselves as pilots were in a permanent state of nerves about our status. Rumour had it that there was a surplus of pilots and that we were to be down graded to navigators (properly called Observers, they wore a single 'Wing' sprouting out of an O, known as a 'flying arsehole'). Worse still we feared being down graded to air gunner—an insult to the bravest of the brave, but all the glamour was attached to being a pilot and that was what we desperately wanted to be.

This may have been an Initial Training Wing, but not a lot of training happened. We did some drill, but whereas in the army drill is a crucial element in the making of a good soldier, in the RAF it was merely a means of getting us into some sort of order on the rare occasions when we were on the parade ground. Corporal Hemmings was in charge of our flight and drilled us from time to time. He regarded me as effeminate and called me 'Ethel'. "Ethel! Get your 'air cut, Ethel!" But Corporal Hemmings was made of softer stuff than the Uxbridge Flight Sergeant and my hair was able to grow a little. Unfortunately, as prospective pilots we were apt to give ourselves airs, but Hemmings had some little jokes designed to keep us in our place:

"Fall out all pilots! I've got some special news for you. Right. Get over to the canteen and clear up that mess you 'orrible lot left last night."

We soon got wise.

We had lectures, but the only one I can recall was by the Medical Officer on the perils of VD. "Only peers and the clergy get VD from lavatory seats." Someone fainted. There were lectures on the history of the RAF and on elementary maths and navigation, and we had to practice the Morse Code, on all of which we had to pass exams. We also had some new-fangled psychological tests for aptitude as pilots, but were assured that we were only guinea pigs and that the results would not affect our future, which we certainly hoped was true.

To begin with the ITW was pretty disorganised, but as time went by—and it went by painfully slowly—things gradually improved. Nevertheless, I was able to spend time with my undergraduate friends who were still in residence. Derek Bolton was still on indefinite leave waiting for an ITW place and living in his comfortable rooms opposite Trinity Great Gate. He was reading engineering so we expected him to become an engineer officer, but as it turned out no such logic could be relied on. (My elder brother, whose only qualifications were as a stockbroker and fluent German speaker, was trained as a fitter, but he was never able to file a piece of metal square. Fortunately for the aircraft the penny soon dropped and he was moved to RAF Technical Intelligence). Anyway, for us there was time to go gliding and riding and to enjoy parties, despite little troubles like dinner at my favourite restaurant in the Arts Theatre costing a week's pay. I enjoyed my double life, although it did mean frequent appeals to my father for funds.

The nearest thing we got to an aircraft was the Link Trainer, an early but effective form of flight simulator. The box sat in the middle of a room, surrounded by a painted landscape as seen from the air. It contained a cockpit with the basic controls and instruments of a real aircraft, to which it responded both in attitude and in the readings on the instruments. It was realistic and particularly so when the hood was closed for blind flying practice. The motion felt all wrong, so we learnt the need to ignore our sensations and rely totally on the instruments. Indeed, so realistic was the Link that I would come out of a blind flying session sweating with fear.

Time still passed far too slowly. It was tedious and frustrating. We seemed no nearer to real aeroplanes, only to increasingly petty regulations enforced by 'penguins' (officers with no 'Wings'). In Western Europe nothing happened either until May 1940, when the Germans attacked Belgium and Holland, and things began to hot up. A letter to my mother dated 10 May said: "All leave is cancelled. In other words the RAF is in a panic"; but still nothing much happened for several more days, although rumours were rife.

Then suddenly, after five frustrating months, No.1 ITW came to life. We were all posted out in a series of dramatic moves which started at 5pm with a telephone message that we were confined to barracks. Throughout that night the action went on. We had medical inspections; we were issued with special kit; we handed in other kit and we were paid. Finally, at eight the next morning we marched to the railway station from which, in a series of three uncomfortable trains, we rattled our way to Doncaster. From there we went on to RAF Finningley, but it was a mistake and after a miserable night we were sent back to RAF Doncaster, where we arrived thoroughly browned off and discouraged.

The idea was that aircrew awaiting flying training should go to operational stations and there absorb whatever they could about the business of the war in the air, but Doncaster was a converted civil airfield, occupied by a transport squadron, and we were out of luck. One day, however, some of us hitched a lift to Hemswell, the nearby bomber station to which some of our Downing friends had been posted. It was a revelation. Here were real aeroplanes, Handley Page Hampdens, with real guns sticking out, and there were officers who were not penguins. I was amazed and delighted when I saw a pilot officer thumb a lift from a passing truck, toss his gas mask in the back and jump in after it. At No.1 ITW you didn't toss your gas mask, you wore it correctly slung—and anyway it wasn't a gas mask, it was a 'respirator, anti-gas'. Here at last was the real RAF and I was thrilled. I was also envious because our friends who had been sent to Hemswell flew nearly every day as passengers on test flights, had lectures from bomber crews and unlike us were billetted in reasonable comfort.

Back at Doncaster we were given the job of aerodrome defence, together with a motley collection of airmen and local soldiery. They were a roughish lot and a night in the Drill Hall, where we slept on palliasses on the floor, certainly broadened the mind. By now it was June 1940 and as there was an increasing fear of invasion we had to man machine gun posts round the airfield night and day to guard against enemy aircraft or parachutists. We were also issued with rifles. They dated from World War I and had been packed ever since in grease, but once cleaned they were perfectly good, as I discovered.

At school rifle shooting had been my thing. It was a way of getting out of cricket, which I hated, so I knew something about the handling of firearms, unlike some of my companions. It was bad enough to see loaded rifles vaguely pointed in any direction, but one night, while asleep in the guard room during during a twenty four hour spell of duty, I woke to the sound of a rifle shot and saw an airman with a vacant expression on his face holding a smoking rifle (not that rifles actually smoke). There was consternation all round, but the bullet had fortunately ploughed horizontally through a table top and hurt no one. All the same the war was becoming dangerous.

We had firing practice on a twenty five yards range on the station, where I found that my rifle sights needed a correction from the normal setting. One day we were taken for firing on a two hundred yards range, under instruction from the Army. When we were all lying down and ready a Sergeant issued the ammunition and explained how to set the sights for two hundred yards, but I was determined to know better and set mine with the correction I reckoned was necessary. It was a large correction and when a Captain came along checking each of us it stuck out a mile.

"This airman here, Sergeant. Sights not set correctly."

The sergeant again explained to me how to set the sights and I explained to him that there was a zero error. The Captain fumed. Then in a rash moment I said:

"Just let me do it my way and I guarantee to put every shot through the bull."

Arrogant, and worse still, foolhardy, for I had only managed this feat two or three times in my life. I began to regret my folly, but when the order came to fire: bang! the first shot was signalled a bull, and the second, and the third, and finally all of them. One of those angels who watch over fools must have been hovering overhead. The Captain, a sort of Army style penguin, retreated in disgust, while the Sergeant, who maybe did not think much of penguins, was delighted and congratulated me warmly as soon as he decently could. It made my day.

We continued with our guard duty, twenty four hours on and twenty four hours off, although not all the time in the machine gun posts. It was tedious, waiting hour after hour for an enemy who was unlikely to appear, but if he did would probably catch us napping. One day we were indeed caught, although not exactly by the enemy; and as I described it in a letter:

I have often heard it said that our Wing Commander is mad, now I fully believe it. He dashed up in his car to the gun post a few evenings ago and leapt out. "Get the cover off that gun. Come on, it should be off by now." Then he leapt up astride the wall of sand bags. "Come on, move; hit 'em, they won't break. Young fellows like you should be able to bite those guns in half with your teeth. Old greybeards like me can't do it." He then leapt down again and started on the sentry outside. "I want you to get these men to crouch down like this and peer all round"—with suitable comic demonstrations—"and when the beggars come, wait, wait until you can see the whites of their eyes. Then get 'em, get 'em between the eyes, they're better dead."

Well, maybe he had a point and certainly at that time everyone was trembling in anticipation of invasion, except for the machine gun crews at RAF Doncaster, who were probably half asleep. All the same it was a lesson for the future; a night fighter could creep up on you just as stealthily.

The guns in question were Lewis guns—primitive World War I things—but at Doncaster we were also introduced to the latest Browning gun and were taught how to strip and reassemble its complicated mechanism and even to do it blindfold. The Browning was the main armament of RAF aircraft in the early part of the war and was formidable, firing a thousand rounds a minute. Spitfires and Hurricanes carried eight of them.

There was a transport squadron at Doncaster which had a motley collection of aircraft, including some elderly Handley Page 42s, commandeered from Imperial Airways. These were the vast four engined biplanes which before the war plied between Croydon and Paris carrying forty passengers at a stately speed of less than 100 mph, but in elegant luxury. One day some of us were taken as ballast on a test flight in one of these monsters, but gone were the elegant fittings and gone too was the refined handling by the airline pilots. On landing we bumped and bounced our way across the airfield with everything bending and shaking, but nothing broke and I survived my first flight with the RAF.

On 4 June we each received a letter from No.1 ITW saying that we had not been forgotten and would soon be posted to a flying school, which was thoughtful of them as forgotten was just what we felt. A few days later some lucky ones left; then after two more seemingly interminable weeks came the great moment when I was posted to No.22 Elementary Flying Training School.

CHAPTER TWO

Flying Training at Last

No.22 Elementary Flying Training School

AT last, nine long months after I had applied to join the RAF, I arrived at No.22 EFTS and found myself back once more at Cambridge, this time at Marshall's Aerodrome. Before the war it had been the civil airfield for Cambridge where we had sometimes flown our gliders, using the hot air from the neighbouring cement works to keep us up. Apart from the instructors, a few administrative people and some airmen for guard duties, it was still run by civilians and was by far the most comfortable place I had been in. The food was good and, although only airmen, we even had waiters in the mess; there was a pupils' lounge and good sleeping quarters. The course was for only eight weeks, so we were worked hard, with very little time off, but that didn't worry us, because at last we were flying. We had lectures on navigation, armament, airmanship, signals, ship and aircraft recognition, parachutes and Service Law and Administration—but rows of Tiger Moths waited for us every morning, and that was what we had really come for.

By now the 'Phoney War' had well and truly ended. The evacuation from Dunkirk was over by 2 June, though the battle for France was still raging, but we pupils paid no heed to the war outside. Our attention was concentrated on the all-absorbing job of learning to fly, of getting our 'Wings', of becoming RAF pilots—and at all costs not being down graded. I began with thirty minutes' dual instruction from Pilot Officer Russell, who remained my instructor throughout the course. He was young and sympathetic and to me he was not far off a god. He taught me to fly and—even better—to fly properly. Only two days after arrival I wrote home with this description of a day in the life on an EFTS pupil:

Dear Pop
Average day seems to pass more or less as follows. Get up, breakfast and what not between about seven and eight fifteen. At eight fifteen parade and more or less promptly get

dismissed and go and get Sidcot outer, helmet and goggles, go get a parachute. Then carry all this, which is very heavy, out onto the aerodrome and look for the instructor. One then flies about in a Tiger Moth. This morning for instance we took off, flew most of the way to Ely and practiced a few turns, then we did gliding turns down to horrible lowth. Whereupon he has the disconcerting habit of saying: "Right, now put the engine on and fly back to the aerodrome." Admittedly I have never failed to find it yet, but you tend to get a bit lost, especially as it is very shrewdly camouflaged. Followed a few circuits and landings which were moderately successful. All that occupied an hour. Flights vary between an hour and half an hour.

We now take half an hour for refreshments, when the officers are to be found in the pupils' mess. Then we go out again and fly out to Caxton, of gliding history, and land there. This piece of navigation I accomplish successfully, but make a mess of landing owing largely to not being able to see which way the wind is blowing. We then fly back to Cambridge, climbing all the way, and arrive at some four thousand feet where we practice "action in the event of fire". To wit, we switch off the petrol and open the throttle, we side slip away from the fire. The engine stops and we switch it off. The fire gets worse and worse so we prepare to bale out. We do not bale out; instead we restart the engine by standing the thing on its nose until it achieves some hundred and fifty miles an hour.[1] We go and land.

At seven o'clock we dine. From eight till nine thirty we have compulsory study on certain nights. Later we go to bed. Later there is an air raid warning, we go to sleep. Later still there is a man who tells us to go to the air raid shelters. We get a rifle and go there. We stand outside. A lot of search-lights shine, some gunfire in the distance. We are told to go back to bed, we go to sleep. A Heinkel flies over, behind it is Spitfire. It drops a bomb. The bomb kills several people in Cambridge. The Spitfire kills the Heinkel. It crashes the other side of the aerodrome. We are still asleep. Had any parachutists descended we would have taken our rifles and machine guns and killed them.

Yours, Walter.

---

[1] Actually, I recall that Russell's instructions for restarting the engine were: "Now we dive like shit!"

Our early lessons were mostly simple circuits and bumps, with climbing, gliding, straight and level (not so easy), and turns ('don't let the nose drop'). Take off was easy. The aircraft was moving into its natural element and so as long as I could keep it more or less straight until I had flying speed I was away. But landings were more difficult. I had to be in the right place, at the right speed and at the right time. This meant that when the aircraft was just inside the boundary and a foot or so above the ground it must lose flying speed, so that it would sink gently onto the ground, main wheels and tail wheel together. If I came in too fast the Tiger refused to be forced onto the ground and went bouncing all across the field. Luckily, flying an aeroplane did not seem so very different from flying a glider, and there was plenty of gliding to be done because the drill for approach and landing was to join the circuit at a thousand feet, close the throttle and not touch it again until after landing.

Circuits and bumps all day were not very good for the instructor's nerves. The pupil was most likely to come to grief on take off and landing, and flying round the circuit were often a dozen Tigers and other aircraft, with no air traffic control. *Punch* published a poem at that time, "The Flying Instructor's Lament", whose first verse went:

> 'What did you do in the war, Daddy?
> How did you help us to win?
> Circuits and bumps and turns, laddie,
> And how to get out of a spin.'

Anyway, Russell's nerves survived the strain, and after eight hours' dual he sent me off solo in the Tiger. Of course I had flown solo in gliders, because in those days you went solo from the very first hop, but there was something breathtaking about my first solo in an aeroplane. It was a loss of virginity, after which the world could never be quite the same again. In a way it was like all those things which you want to do, but hang back from, half afraid to commit yourself—walking to the edge of the diving board, or making a speech; or like those things which you don't want to do but know that you must—walking into the headmaster's study, telling someone of their friend's death. You hesitate, then something clicks, and you push the throttle open and go.

Come to think of it, it must be like that as you walk towards the gallows.

The lessons continued: loops, spins, slow rolls, cross countries, blind flying. But there was also a different lesson which the CO put on whenever a new course arrived. There were a number of Gloster Gladiators on the station for which Marshalls did the overhauls. They were the last of the biplane fighters and soon to be consigned to museums, though a few were still on active service, particularly the famous 'Faith', 'Hope' and 'Charity' in Malta. The CO would take up one of the Gladiators and give the new pupils an electrifying display of low level aerobatics. For us it was strictly forbidden, but the lesson was unmistakeable: 'When you have flown a few thousand hours and can fly like me, maybe you can do that sort of thing, but if you try now I shall not even need to have you on the mat, because I shall be writing to your parents deeply regretting that their son was killed during flying training.'

We had to pass three flying tests, one with the Flight Commander, one with the CO, and finally—and most dreaded of all—the 'RAF Test', conducted by an independent officer. My first test went okay, and Flight Lieutenant Richardson said: "Your instrument flying and aerobatics are very good." After most of the manoeuvres on the next test the CO murmured: "Yes, very nice." So far, so good. But the RAF Test was yet to come. The testing officer was a F/Lt Slade, known as 'The Black Butcher', not only because he wore black overalls, but because he had no hesitation in failing anyone who fell short of his high standards. Failure meant the end of flying as a pilot, and we knew a good many who had failed already at the hands of the Black Butcher. The dreaded day came on 17 July, the course having been cut to five weeks because of the increasing shortage of pilots. I climbed apprehensively into the cockpit behind Slade and taxied out, still fearful of making a mess of the whole thing, but after take off my worries faded as everything seemed to go well enough. Finally, Slade's voice came over the intercom: "Do a slow roll." This was it. Slow rolls were difficult to execute elegantly, especially in a slow biplane, but there was no escape. Check the straps are tight, pick up some extra speed, then raise the nose a little and roll to starboard. Keep it straight at all costs. Keep rolling. Upside down now. Hold the nose up—or is it down? The ground is where the sky ought to be. Mud from the floor falls in my face. The engine cuts out. Keep the nose up. Keep going, right over and up the other side. Still straight and level. Thank God. The engine restarts as petrol flows back into the carburettor and Slade's voice comes again: "Hm. Not bad." Praise indeed from the Black Butcher. Then: "Okay, I've got her. We'll go back and land." Saved again, as I was none too confident of making a Slade class landing. The course was over. I had done fifty five hours flying and passed out 'Above Average'. They had apparently toyed with 'Exceptional', but I didn't quite make it.

During the fine summer of 1940 the war was hotting up. France fell and Germany now ruled from the north of Norway to the Spanish frontier. Bombing raids were building up against Britain, but still I have no recollection that we pupils felt involved. The fields and skies of Cambridgeshire were still peaceful and our flying was all absorbing.

There was little time to get to know the other pupils on the course, except for one who had become a close friend. He was Walter Rusk, older than most of us and a notable racing motor-cyclist. Blond. Irish. A character. I rode pillion behind him one day on a borrowed dispatch rider's bike and it seemed the safest thing I had ever done. He was totally in control. A real professional. One day he showed me a picture of his girlfriend. She was sitting on a bed and on the card she had written: "I'm wearing my new dress. It buttons down the front and I think you'll like it." I do not suppose Walter ever got the chance to unbutton it, for shortly after we were both posted to No. 7 Flying Training School he was killed.

No.7 Flying Training School, Peterborough

I was now officially a 'Pilot under Training' and proudly wrote to my father instructing him to address me as 'LAC Morison, Pilot U/T'. On 20 July ten of us travelled from Cambridge to Peterborough. This was an RAF station, but it was shared with the Fleet Air Arm. The Navy flew Fairey Battles, large single engined monoplane bombers, while we flew Hawker Hart biplanes. The Hart was the last of the light bombers of the thirties and had seen most of its service curbing unruly tribesmen on the North West Frontier and thereabouts, but to us it was a real fighting aeroplane, even if a relic from another age, and much more exciting to fly than a Tiger. It may have been intended as a bomber, but there was nothing you could not do with a Hart. At the same time it was a simple aeroplane, with fixed undercarriage, fixed-pitch prop, no flaps and no supercharger. Unlike the Tiger it did at least have wheel brakes, although they did not actually do much good, so that landings still had to be nicely judged. Sergeant Balchin was my instructor, and without delay we launched into a course designed to last three and a half months and cover just about everything: aerobatics, spins, gunnery, bombing, navigation, reconnaissance, form-ation flying, night flying, blind flying. One thing, however, it mercifully did not include—as we found out when we were having an introductory lecture from the Chief Ground Instructor, a Naval Lieutenant Commander.

"Sir," said someone. "What about PT?"

"PT?" said the old sea dog. "Good God, we haven't got time for that sort of thing here."—and there never did seem to be time for it in the RAF.

Many of the lessons were new; not least night flying, which fascinated me. The blacked out land below was no longer patterned with the lights of towns and little glow worms of vehicles marking out the roads. Now it was completely dark to frustrate prowling German intruders. On the little grass field of our satellite at Sibson, where we did the night flying, we had a dim flare path of portable 'glim lamps'—things with no more than the power of a pocket torch--plus a couple of paraffin flares to mark the upwind end and give just enough light to locate the airfield from a distance. Well, not much of a distance. Even on moonless nights there was usually a little light in the sky—enough to see a horizon—but with no moon and thick cloud the darkness was absolute. Floating alone up there, with nothing visible but a dim glow from the instruments and a little flame from the exhausts, one felt detached from the world. Even the thin life line of the flare path had a disturbing way, when you banked the aircraft, of appearing to be up in the sky instead of on the ground where it belonged. Then, if you got your approach right, you had it straight in front of you, the glim lamps flashed past and you landed on ground you could not see: altogether a breath taking experience. Air raid warnings brought flying to a halt and were quite a problem if you were airborne when the warning came. A red signal lamp was flashed at any aircraft in the air and you tried to get down before they put the flare path out, but if not you stayed in the air until the 'All Clear'. One night I got down just as all the lights went out and it was so dark that I couldn't see which way to go, so for fear of taxiing into something, I left the Hart standing where we had stopped and wandered about the field groping for the Nissen hut, which was the only building on the field.

Real blind flying, in cloud, and not just under the hood, was more exhausting than exciting and lacked the thrill of night flying. With no horizon I could see nothing see except my own wings in a damp grey mist, the senses tried to mislead and the lesson was to learn total faith in the instruments. The Harts we flew did not even have the luxury of an artificial horizon to make it relatively easy. Everything had to be inferred from the turn and bank indicator—not that it actually told you which way you were banked—and from the airspeed indicator and altimeter. In the Link trainer at Downing the battle to believe the instruments had left me sweating and now the real thing was even more shattering. A rising scream warned that I was heading for the ground fast, while a horrible hush and soggy controls meant I was about to stall. But in the end it was all worth while when I could climb up through solid cloud to play alone around brilliant sunlit cumulus tops, like gigantic snow mountains, solid looking, but wraith-like when I dived back into them.

Soon we were being sent on quite long cross country flights, such as a hundred miles or so via Leighton Buzzard and Cheltenham and back to Peterborough. One day, when I was supposed to be doing some boring navigation exercise, I made an unofficial diversion to Caxton, the satellite to our EFTS at Cambridge, where I saw a Tiger, flying high above the field. He gave chase so we pursued each other's tails for a while, pretending to be fighter pilots, and because this was scarcely the expected behaviour of an EFTS pupil I assumed he must be one of the instructors. I landed, hoping that he would too and that we might renew old acquaintance, but on the ground I was confronted by a furious instructor. He accused me of beating up his pupil and threatened to report me to my unit. I was terrified of collecting any black marks which might get me taken off flying, but mercifully he relented and I scuttled back to Peterborough, thankful for my escape.

At Peterborough we lived in airmen's barrack huts, which were reasonably comfortable, but soon after we had started the advanced course, life suddenly took a turn for the better. We were issued with white arm bands and told that we would now live in the officers' mess. We had wondered whether we would be officer cadets, but the RAF did not recognise the existence of such creatures. When we asked what we were no one quite seemed to know, but why worry about titles when we had all the comforts?—we did not even need a pass to go on leave, just the flight commander's permission and a signature in the signing out book in the mess. This privilege nearly led me into more trouble. Cambridge was within easy hitch hiking distance and I kept drifting off there because many friends were still around, among them Derek on seemingly interminable leave. (Soon afterwards he was posted to the ITW at Aberystwyth, a place he didn't care for and which he referred to derisively as 'Aberysmal'.) On one weekend leave I returned to Cambridge and had an alcoholic evening party with friends, but made the great mistake of drinking much too much sherry (not a wise thing at the best of times). When at last I realised that I must depart if I was to get a train back to Peterborough in time to fly the next morning I was very drunk. It was also very late, and when I tottered out into Jesus Lane I walked straight into the arms of two RAF Police, who asked sharply what I was doing.

"I'm on leave."

"Show us your pass."

"I haven't got a pass."

Trying desperately to appear sober, I explained about the signing out book in the mess, but they must have thought the world had turned upside down. An LAC in the officers' mess? Impossible! Anyway, after taking my name and unit, they let me go, drunk, but fortunately not too disorderly. I had blotted my copy book, and had visions of being taken off flying—no 'Wings', no commission. I also had a splitting headache and a ghastly train journey which seemed to last all night and trail all round East Anglia. Finally, as I dragged myself back through the deserted streets of Peterborough in the early dawn a German aircraft dropped three bombs. At least they did not hit me, although at the time it seemed small consolation. That morning I suffered the agony of having to do a navigation test with Sgt Balchin. I'd had no sleep and still had a raging headache, but feared the headache could turn out to be the least of my punishments.

I waited apprehensively for my sins to catch up with me until, a day or two later, just as I was going out to my aircraft, an orderly appeared on a bicycle.

"LAC Morison?" he asked.

"Yes."

"The station commander wants to see you."

Sinking feeling. "When?"

""E says at your convenience. Not to interfere with your flying."

Well, that sounded strange, but a bit more hopeful and so, as soon as I could, I hurried to his office. The CO was a fatherly figure, reputed to be the oldest Group Captain in the service, and as I entered and saluted he looked up from his desk.

"Who is it? Ah. Morison. Yes–Um–Er–Yes. Let me see. ..Ah yes! Here it is–a report here from a Corporal...er...: Smith of the Service Police. It says that at 22.45 hours on the night of the 15th instant you were seen in Jesus Lane, Cambridge, without a pass, not wearing your cap field service and wearing your respirator anti-gas incorrectly slung. Er... now tell me Morison, could that be right do you think?" (Nothing about being drunk, so perhaps things weren't too bad after all.)

"Well, Sir. Yes, Sir. It could be right, Sir."

"Um. Now this Corporal...er...Smith–would you say, Morison, that perhaps he was being–how shall I put it– somewhat over zealous?"

"Well, Sir. Yes, Sir. I suppose you might say that."

"Well, thank you Morison. That will be all. Oh, and by the way, good luck."

A wise old man, and not so old I suppose, but to me at twenty he seemed aged. I saluted smartly and escaped, unable to believe my good fortune–and have admired the old gentleman's tactfulness ever since.

This was the time of the Blitz on London and I only realised how peaceful it was in Peterborough when I went home to see my parents. I found myself quivering in the air raid shelter, not even able to tell the difference between our own guns and bursting bombs, while the Londoners, who had got used to it, took no notice. At Peterborough there were plenty of warnings, but they mostly came to nothing. Then one day there was a scare about a German landing on the coast, which gave us a lot of excitement because we longed to fly the Harts and Battles and bomb the invaders. The rumour was that a squadron of Blenheims had blown the barges out of the water, but the truth was that it was just a rumour.

By the time we reached the advanced course at Peterborough we had mastered all the basics of handling the Hart and now did more in the way of bombing and shooting. We did low level and dive bombing. We were not quite like Stukas, as we had no dive brakes, but we dived steeply from 5000 to 2000 feet before releasing practice bombs onto targets out in The Wash. For gunnery the aircraft were fitted with telescopic sights, which might have been ideal for a sniper's rifle but could not have been less suitable in an aircraft. The new reflector sights fitted to Hurricanes and Spitfires used some clever optical trick to make a red ring appear in the air out in front of the aircraft and apparently to surround the target, so that the pilot could keep his eyes focussed on it, uninterupted by having to look through sights close in front of his nose. When you looked through the Hart's telescopic sight the field of view was tiny and everything else was out of focus. This made diving on a ground target quite an adventure, because so long as you were looking through the sight you had little idea of how low you were getting and with enthusiasm might get too low. Nevertheless, I survived, and my bombing and shooting scores were mostly above average. Another exercise was to climb to 15,000 feet with a full bomb load and without oxygen. Fifteen thousand feet is almost three miles and the first time alone at that height I felt a long way from my fellow men. Shortage of oxygen creates euphoria, or so they tell you, but I can't say that I noticed it and I was glad to throttle back and start my descent.

So the course went on without any great drama—apart from the tragedy when Walter Rusk was killed. He had dived steeply into the ground, for no apparent reason, but Walter was one who liked to push things to the limit and so maybe he had pushed the Hart too far. He was the first of my friends to go and his death cast a gloom over all of us. Fortunately, other local excitements did not end in disaster. A Wellington landed on the airfield with its undercarriage collapsed, but no one was hurt. A Naval pupil in a Battle found he could only get one wheel down as he came in to land and a crowd collected to see what would happen; his instructor was about to take off in another aircraft to try and guide him down as gently as possible, but as we all held our breath, he made an almost perfect landing on the one wheel and became the hero of the day.   A few days later a Hurricane landed with a failing engine, which gave us the chance to keep the pilot up half the night in the mess to find out what the war was all about, but without a lot of success.

Towards the end of October I had passed all the flying tests and was told that because my flying was above average I was to go on to the Central Flying School to become an instructor.   This made me reasonably happy because the CFS would put a real polish on my flying, though what I really wanted was to go on to fighters.   The Battle of Britain had been fought during August and September, ending with the Hurricane and Spitfire squadrons in the south east of England breaking the Luftwaffe offensive, and so my heroes were fighter pilots.   Above all I wanted to fly Spitfires.

Came 8 November.   The course was finished and finally I was Pilot Officer Morison.   Then came the blow.   My instructor said: "With your flying you should be going to fighters, but I'm afraid you are going to Army Co-operation." Presumably someone had decided that the urgent need for more fighter pilots had receded, but at the time, soon after the evacuation from Dunkirk, we scarcely had an army in a fit state to fight, so there didn't seem much need for more Army Co-operation pilots either.   Anyway, at least it wasn't Bomber Command.

I now had leave, so off I went to London and to Austin Reeds to buy a Pilot Officer's uniform, complete with those treasured 'Wings'.   Then it was on to RAF Old Sarum, near Salisbury.

The School of Army Co-operation, Old Sarum

I arrived at Old Sarum, within sight of Salisbury cathedral, at the end of November 1941, self-conscious in my new Pilot Officer's uniform, to find myself at an old established RAF station with permanent brick buildings.   We enjoyed the peacetime comforts in the mess, but endured the old established disciplines which still prevailed.   Our job here was to learn the skills required for army co-operation: low level reconnaissance, photography, artillery spotting, ground attack with guns and bombs, dropping and picking up messages, radio communication, both morse and telephone; we even practiced dropping poison gas. All this was splendid practice for any sort of flying, but it was more relevant to World War I than the 1940s.

We flew Westland Lysanders, which were fascinating aircraft; but like the tactics which we learned they too were outdated. Lightly armed with only two Brownings forward and a few small bombs, they could not do much damage. Top speed was not much over 200 mph and with only one gun firing aft they were hopelessly vulnerable. Everyone knew that in France the Messerschmitts had shot them out of the sky, but fortunately the lessons were to sink in before too long; Army Co-operation Command disappeared and was replaced by the Tactical Air Force, which had high speed aircraft armed with cannon, rockets, or a substantial bomb load.

At Old Sarum we enjoyed tearing about the countryside at nought feet trying to report the position of troops or tanks, or more likely hay stacks, because the army was thin on the ground; or flying over the artillery ranges on Salisbury Plain reporting where the shells had landed. After flying we enjoyed a happy social life, either in the mess, or in the 'Haunch of Venison' in Salisbury, where they would always cash a cheque. We also had invitations to splendid parties from County families who wanted to entertain the 'brave boys in blue'.

By midwinter the weather was foul—snow, ice, fog, the lot. We flew through most of it, but sometimes it was impossible and the course was extended for several weeks. However, by the beginning of February I had done it all and was posted out to an Army Co-operation squadron.

241 Squadron, Inverness

On 9 February, 1941, I arrived at 241 Squadron, stationed at Inverness. No.241 had been formed as an offshoot from the City of Cardiff Auxiliary Squadron and many of its people were from that city. Being Welsh they were also Rugby players, and the blackest smear which they could put on your character was that you 'played the Swansea rules'. Luckily, though, they were very friendly to foreigners like me.

I was now on a squadron and all trained to fight, but in the far north of Scotland there didn't seem to be much prospect of that, so we mostly just carried on with training, much as we had at Old Sarum. The only faintly war-like activity was to fly dawn reconnaissances along the coast, looking for any enemy who might have slipped ashore during the night in a rubber dinghy from a U-boat. Not surprisingly we never saw any. However, there was a tiny bit of drama one day when a German aircraft flew over Inverness and on down Loch Ness to drop some bombs on the aluminium smelter at Fort William. We never saw it, though it had evidently attracted attention at Group headquarters, because next day the CO called the squadron together and addressed us with some remarkable words:

"I have received an order from Group. It says that under no circumstances is the squadron to engage any enemy aircraft which may intrude into the area. That is official. But now I have an order for you from myself, which is that if any pilot in my squadron has the opportunity to engage the enemy and fails to do so he needn't bother to land back at this station."

That was a bit more like the Churchill spirit, and as a Spitfire pilot *manqué* I rather fancied myself shooting down a Heinkel with my Lysander, but the chance never came. However, one day when I was sitting quietly in my cockpit on the airfield I did nearly shoot some innocent Scotsmen. The armourer was adjusting my guns and he called out:

"Press the firing button, Sir."

"You're sure they're unloaded?"

"Yes."

"Sure?"

"Yes, Sir. Unloaded."

I pressed. The two Brownings shrieked and the bullets soared away over Inverness. Where they went no one knew, but we had no complaints; maybe they killed the Loch Ness Monster, but I never saw it, dead or alive, despite many flights over the loch.

We lived in the Caledonian Hotel, which was a luxury billet, but Inverness itself was a pretty dour place. For light relief there was an officers' club, run by a Wing Commander in a shack out towards the loch. It was called the 'Hi Diddly Dee' and we had quite a hectic time there, including dancing Scottish reels, which Nick Bateman, one of my Southern friends, complained "savoured of barbarism". Alas, the 'Hi Diddly Dee' did not last long due to some scandal, and the higher military authorities decreed that the Wingco was an unsuitable person to have charge of such an establishment and must give up control. The squadron went in force to a meeting to decide the future of the place and there was much heated debate, but when the auditor said that if the place closed it would cost each of us twenty five shillings to clear the debts we reckoned that it had better close before any more bills came in. However, there was a majority of one in favour of continuing, so next morning we resigned *en masse* and the resignations were delivered forthwith by a dispatch rider.

In the hotel there was a girl who sometimes played the piano and sang for us. There were two songs which I had never heard before, or since, but wish I could hear again. She was a very beautiful girl. I still remember the tunes, but only a few words. One was sentimental:

> 'The badge on your coat
> Will be mine ever more,
> Will be mine to remind me of you.'

The other, which we all sang lustily, may have had a double entendre, I'm not sure:

> 'Swing my conker, let it swing, let it swing.
> Down at the bottom of its string, of its string.
> Hold yours out, let me hit it with mine.
> I bet I'll break your conker every time.'

Ah well. Perhaps it was just a Boy Scouts' song after all.

We got around more than when we were at training stations. One day I had to take a Lysander down to Doncaster to be fitted with two twenty millimetre cannons, to beef up the fire power for ground attack. A second aircraft was going, and as the pilot's family lived near Acklington, where there was an RAF station, we decided to stop there for the night. Before landing we beat up his family home and later, when we went to visit them, they said that I had hit a tree. I didn't believe them, but inspection revealed a nasty dent in the fairing round one of the wheels. This was a blow to my pride and was embarrassing, as you were not supposed to go round hitting things, especially when you were not even on an authorised low flying exercise. All came right, however, because a word with the fitters at Doncaster had the damage repaired before the aircraft was returned to the squadron. Then, when I went to fetch it back, I suffered another blow to my pride, this time as a navigator. Rather than follow roads and railways, which was the squadron's usual habit, I decided to do some proper navigation. Feeling a bit smug, I set a compass course for Grangemouth, near Edinburgh, but after a while the barren hills below began to bear less and less resemblance to what the map indicated. A little voice in my head kept insisting: 'You're lost, you're lost, and you haven't chosen very good weather to get lost in.' I was indeed lost, and when eventually I recognised something on the ground it was miles off my route and near Carlisle, on the wrong side of England. The cause, when it emerged, was that the big new cannons had altered the aircraft's magnetism, but the compass had not been adjusted to compensate for the change and was about twenty five degrees in error. It was a blow to my airmanship also because I should have known to check the compass after such a major refit.

I made another mistake that week, as I took the opportunity in Doncaster to post a letter to my father with the news that we might be moving to Cambridge. I should not have done it, no matter how trivial the information may have seemed nor how discreet I may have believed my father to be, as the North of Scotland was a security area from which all outward mail was censored. The whole country was plastered with posters saying 'Careless Talk Costs Lives', and I had taken no notice.

Among the odd jobs which I had to do was to pay the landladies in the fifty or so houses where our airmen were billetted, and it was gratifying that with only one exception they were pleased to have them and said what nice young men they were. The exception was at a Temperance Hotel where the landlady was rude and asserted that she was being swindled by the RAF. However, there was to be no more of this for me in Inverness as after two months my time with 241 Squadron was up.

In March 1941, although there was fighting in Greece and North Africa, it was remote from home and something was needed to show the much bombed people in Britain that we were fighting back at the Germans and no longer merely defending ourselves against them. A big effort was now to be made to build up Bomber Command and carry the war to the heart of the enemy. Thus it was that on 7 April, together with Pat Doorly and Mike Thomas, both good Cardiff men, I found myself travelling the few miles along the coast of the Moray Firth to Lossiemouth and No.20 Bomber Command Operational Training Unit.

So much for Army Co-operation, and now for Bomber Command, which I had tried so hard to avoid.

CHAPTER THREE

Lossiemouth—No.20 OTU

THE work of this Operational Training Unit (OTU) was to take pilots who had left Flying Training Schools with the basic ability to fly and to teach them how to handle a Wellington. It was also to give the observers and wireless operators experience of long cross country flights, and to train air gunners. We had understood that we were to go through the course, but our welcome at Lossie turned out to be somewhat mixed: "Who are you?" "Where are you from?" "We've never heard of you, and anyway all the courses are full." Then suddenly the tone changed—"Where did you say you've come from?" "Oh. You're from a squadron are you?" "You mean you know how to fly?" "Oh great, then we've got a job for you."—and before we had been there a day we were staff pilots and the job was to fly observers and W/Ops on their long cross countries.

We flew Avro Ansons, nice, simple and safe aeroplanes, but scarcely battle worthy, having only one rather pathetic gun. They had been worked hard by Coastal Command on reconnaissance and now we flew them all over the North of Scotland, out over the North Sea, out to the Hebrides and the Orkneys and over to Northern Ireland. Mostly these flights lasted about three hours and tended to become boring, unless the weather turned foul when, in that mountainous country, they became extremely frightening.

Navigation was mainly by dead reckoning—plotting on the chart your course, speed and estimated wind—and by map reading when you could see the ground. The wireless operator could take bearings on radio beacons, though that was seldom accurate, or he might ask a ground station to take a bearing on a transmission from the aircraft. This was a lot more accurate, but usually when you wanted it most so did everyone else, as they were just as lost in cloud, so there was a long queue. Despite their shortcomings, even the primitive radio bearings were a great comfort if you had not seen the ground for two or three hours; you could be many miles off course, especially with a pupil navigator. Nevertheless, these were conditions in which crews operating over

Germany had to fly, and for much more than three hours, so it was essential experience.

In Scotland the highest ground is Ben Nevis at 4406 feet, a figure which lives in my head. Above that height in cloud you were safe, but when you had to come down you badly wanted to know just what was underneath. As Lossie was on the coast you could usually be reasonably sure of letting down over the sea, but it was to be another year before more precise radio aids were available and two years before H2S radar. This depicted the ground below and together with Oboe, a radio beam of great accuracy, led at last to the accurate marking of bombing targets. In the meantime, if you wanted to stay alive, you did not rely solely on the navigation of a pupil crew, but kept track of where you were as best you could with your own map. In time I got to know the North of Scotland so well that often the glimpse of a single familiar feature through a hole in the cloud told me where we were. Meanwhile the navigator, poring over his chart, had often calculated that we were somewhere else, and probably suspected me of unfair influence when I proved to be right. Some pupils were not slow to criticize the pilot instead of their own navigation. One even had the temerity to enter in his log: "Pilot continually flying left wing low, causing drift to port."(!)

Lossiemouth had a satellite field about six miles away, near Elgin, and that was where our flight was based. It was called Bogs of Mayne and often lived up to its name. When I arrived there was no mess in Elgin and we were all billetted out. For a short while Pat, Mike and I lived in an hotel, but then the police found us a miracle in the shape of a Miss Reid, a maiden lady who was something of an invalid and lived in a large house in the town called Brae Birnie. She had a cook-housekeeper, three maids and a gardener and we had a room each, with running H & C and bath soap by Morny of Regent Street. We also had a sitting room complete with wireless and quite a library. We were fed superbly, at whatever time we liked, and were given hot cocoa and cakes when we came in from night flying.

Miss Reid spent much of her time in bed, being very frail and looking as though she couldn't be much longer for this world. Then one day I was nearly the death of her when, with total tactlessness, I told her baldly that Pat Doorly had hit a mountainside the previous night while flying in cloud

An Avro Anson. Drawn by a member of 'A' Flight.

and that he and his crew were all dead. Not so long afterwards Mike was killed also, but by then I had learnt to give this sort of news more gently.

If a flight was boring I sometimes played little games to amuse myself. One night when approaching the airfield at a fair height, and while still a few miles short of it, I closed the throttles and decided to try to finish the trip without using the engines again. We glided down for maybe five or ten minutes and everything seemed nicely judged until, when I was down to a couple of hundred feet, I needed just a touch of engine to get in safely, but when I pushed open the throttles absolutely nothing happened. No response. Mercifully we staggered over the boundary and flopped onto the ground a few yards from the perimeter, where both engines stopped dead and I had the embarrassment of needing a ground crew to come and restart them. Then I had to explain to the Flight Commander what the hell I was doing. I had been so absorbed with my little game that I had forgotten to check the tanks. After about three hours they ran dry and you had to switch to another set, which was something you did before starting an approach and not as you crossed the boundary. I couldn't have been more careless and only undeserved luck had saved us. It was a timely lesson.

The luxury at Miss Reid's lasted a couple of months, but then we got a mess in Elgin—a big house in Victorian Gothic style called Blackfriars Haugh. It was rather splendid and had gardens bordering on the River Lossie where, if you were a fisherman like me, you got frustrated watching the salmon swimming round when the water was low. The airmen were still billetted out in the town and one day I went with my Flight Commander, Squadron Leader Piper, to search for more billets. At one house we rang the bell, but when a woman came to the door Piper immediately made an excuse and we left.

"What was wrong with that place, Sir?" I asked.

"Stank of cats. I won't have my men living in a place that stinks of cats."

We were worked hard at Elgin (Bogs of Mayne was now called Elgin) and it was wearing. In May I flew on twenty six days and on nine of them did a night trip as well. Three hours in the air meant much longer from the time you left the flight hut to the time you got back, and sometimes the weather added unwelcome hazards. Ice. Turbulence. Electrical storms.

Occasionally we had flights which were interesting, and more productive than just stooging round the old familiar routes. We might oblige a fighter squadron stationed in the Orkneys by flying one of their people on leave, or by carrying some piece of equipment for their mess which was too big to go in a Hurricane. By way of thanks they would give us a few eggs, which were plentiful in the Orkneys, but scarce on the mainland. Then one day we took the initiative and telephoned their Mess Secretary:

"Could you let us have a few eggs if we came up in an Anson?"

"Sure. How many do you want? A gross? Two gross? Have as many as you like."

Suddenly we became wholesale egg importers and many

there were who kept their fingers crossed for a smooth landing as the Anson touched down at Elgin carrying several crates of eggs. I took a whole crate home to London one day when I went on leave and got some very strange looks on Euston station from people who were probably lucky to get a single egg a week.

One trip I did was unique. Early in the morning I was in the flight office when the phone rang and on the line was the Station Adjutant at Lossie:

"Could you send over an aircraft at once, with a crew prepared to fly to Yorkshire?"

As I was the only pilot available I gathered a crew of pupils, flew over to Lossie and reported to the Adjutant.

"Ah yes, Morison. Now listen. I want you to fly to RAF Holme—it's in Yorkshire you know—and when you get there deliver this hamper to the Commander-in-Chief, Bomber Command, who'll be there on a tour of inspection. It...er...it contains lobsters." (You could tell that from the smell anyway.) "Oh! and...er...take this packet of matches, too, will you?"

"Matches, Sir? In an aircraft, Sir?" (*Strictly forbidden.*)

"Er...well, yes. For the C-in-C, you understand."

"Yes, Sir."

To keep on the right side of the C-in-C was important, so we got airborne, turned south and climbed away toward the four thousand foot peaks of the Cairngorms, heading for Yorkshire.

Holme proved to be a raw new airfield, still incomplete, and no sooner had we landed than the C-in-C arrived in his massive four engined Halifax, together with a considerable retinue. But then came the problem: how could I break through this entourage and deliver a hamper of lobsters to such an exalted personage, busy with his inspection? I hovered on the fringe, but lunch time came and the C-in-C departed to the mess, still surrounded by his aides. As I hadn't yet succeeded in my mission I followed him in. The C-in-C had lunch, and so I had lunch too. As soon as he had finished he hurried out to continue his inspection and I became desperate. He got into his car. In a moment all would be lost, so I pushed my way to the front, saluted smartly and said:

"Excuse me, Sir. I've got your lobsters."

The retinue began to cluck.

"Lobsters?"

"Yes, Sir. From Lossiemouth, Sir. What shall I do with them?"

"Oh yes. Very good. Just put them in my aircraft, will you?"

The retinue clucked louder and shuffled me out of the way.

Mission acomplished, we headed back to Elgin. We had not just been wasting petrol to please a senior officer. It was better experience for the pupil crew than flogging the Anson round the old familiar routes.

At Lossie we flew at night without lights, except when on the circuit, otherwise we would have been sitting ducks for any marauding enemy night fighter. I never heard of a collision, although one night the dark shape of what looked like a Whitley from the OTU at neighbouring Kinloss flashed past, going in the opposite direction. There was no air traffic control, so at night or in cloud a collision would have been pure chance, though we never gave it a second thought. Anyway, as Nick Bateman commented the next day:

"Yes old boy, but you can come a hell of a near without actually hitting someone."

Nick had followed us from 241. He was the one who had condemned Scottish reels for "savouring of barbarism".

Night trips could be full of fascination: moonlight on a sea of clouds, or maybe the Northern Lights. In summer time, flying in the clear air above the clouds, we would sometimes see the northern horizon glowing with this dim, ghostly light, pulsating with great fingers which rose and fell majestically in the sky. Another electrical display which we often saw was St Elmo's Fire, so called because it plays round the mastheads of ships and St Elmo is the patron saint of sailors, in the Mediterranean anyway. It is an eerie blue light caused by electrical brush discharge and sometimes, when we were flying through thunder clouds, it would appear, first as a circle at the propeller tips, then streaming back over the wings like a blue river—spectacular, but harmless.

After a while our flight got some Wellingtons, the aircraft which were the mainstay of Bomber Command until the arrival of the big four engined bombers. Designed by Barnes Wallis, whose fertile mind also produced the bouncing bombs which destroyed the Mohne and Eder dams, they were known affectionately as Wimpeys, presumably after the popular cartoon character of the day, J Wellington Wimpey. I was given a couple of brief flights, dual, and was then away. The Wimpey was an altogether different aircraft from the kindly Anson, bigger, faster and more comfortable, but there was also a feeling of majestic solidity about the way it flew, or so it seemed at first. Faster than an Anson it may have been, but that was relative. The Wimpey cruised at about 140 knots and with a bomb load had a ceiling not much above 15,000 feet, a performance which by this stage in the war was becoming homicidal.

Up to now I had never been more than a temporary resident on any of my stations, but I was at Lossie for over a year. I became part of the establishment and made many friends, though sadly some of them all too briefly—like Henry Hall, one of my flight commanders, a big and kindly man, who was posted back to operations and killed over Denmark; and like Polly Parsons, another flight commander who went the same way as Henry.

There was P/O Berry. As we rode out to the aircraft in a truck with a WAAF driver he called out: "That's my aircraft, Miss. Over there, Miss. It's Haitch. Haitch for Harsehole, Miss." Then there was P/O Blanks, with a coarse sense of humour, phoning his landlady from the mess: "Telephone engineer here, Madam. Testing your line. Will you please repeat after me 'I cannot eat my little currant bun'? Yes, Madam, just testing. Yes, currant bun, Madam." A pause. She was suspicious, but in the end she fell for it. "Then stuff it up your arse, Madam." A shriek emerged from the phone: "*MISTER* Blanks!" He had been recognised.

P/O Grimston was one of a family of earls. He had quite a different sense of humour, and was so tall he could scarcely get into an aircraft. He didn't survive the war either.

There was the Padre. His manners were a bit rough too. He liked his beer, and one night as he went in to a formal mess dinner he sat straight down and called the steward to order a pint. The CO, still standing, admonished him: "Padre, please—grace if you don't mind." The Padre stood up, said: "Thank God," and sat down again. One day he was in the mess with his beer, having just returned from visiting an airman in the cells: "Been to see young Smith. Very sad case, very sad indeed. Standing in the window of his billet and waving his cock at the WAAFs as they walked by."

We all thought Sergeant Wilsher the scruffiest pilot on the station, but one day, after I had landed in a blinding blizzard, he enquired: "Was it you brought that Anson in just now?" "Yes, why?" "Hm. Not bad." Suddenly he did not seem scruffy any more, and just then I felt as if he had awarded me the DFC. I hope he survived the war.

Neville Booth. We shared a room. He had an MG called 'Francisco', after General Franco, but despite this evidence of fascist leanings he was impatient to see action against the Nazis. While on leave he begged a ride with Henry Hall on his fatal trip to Denmark and was killed.

Francis Doyle showed me how to fly a Wimpey. I cannot extract a picture of Francis from my memory, but I can see his wife Sheila all too clearly. Francis was posted to operations and went missing while Sheila was still at Lossie. She was small and beautiful and very sad.

I can remember these friends because they were on the staff, but the pupils came and went too quickly. Where are they now: Sgt Baker and P/O Moore and Sgt Handley and the hundred others I taught to fly Wimpeys? The chances are that few survived.

I was given another unusual trip when I had to deliver a Wellington to Tempsford, an RAF station near Bedford. It sounded simple enough, but when we landed it was to an extremely hostile reception:

"What are you doing here? You can't stay. Get out—and get out fast."

I protested that my instructions were to deliver the aircraft to them, but to no effect, and so we got back into the air and then wondered where to go next. My navigator pressed me to go to Hendon so as to be almost in London, but I wasn't having it:

"I am *NOT* going to Hendon. It's getting dark, it's misty, and there will be barrage balloons everywhere."

"Don't worry Mr Morison, Sir. I'll get you there. I live at Hendon. I know it."

He was an instructor and a first class navigator, but we had no wireless operator and I had no intention of floundering about unannounced among the London defences, so we went to Hatfield. There a red Verey light was fired at us as we approached. Another not very kindly reception, but by now we were getting a bit desperate and in front of us was a perfectly good runway, so we ignored the warning and landed. This time we were allowed to stay the night; and the next day, as we were due a couple of days leave, I sent the crew off and, having made sure that I would be welcome, flew solo to Tempsford.

Why all the fuss the previous evening? I never found out at the time, but the truth was that clandestine operations were carried out from Tempsford and my brother had an almost equally cool reception there later, despite having arranged in advance a visit with his 'Flying Circus'. This was a group of captured German aircraft which he had assembled in the course of his duties in RAF Technical Intelligence, including a Heinkel III, Junkers 88, Messerschmitt 109 and a Focke Wulf 190. He took them to RAF stations to demonstrate their capabilities. When on passage they had a Fighter Command escort, but even so they had some dodgy moments.[1]

At Elgin we shared the airfield with a Hurricane squadron and I eyed their aircraft with envy, as did Neville Booth who, like me, wished he was in Fighter Command. We kept wondering how to get airborne in a Hurricane, but my chance came when their CO, who looked like the Emperor Haile Selassie, approached me in the mess one day:

"I say, Morison, I know this is a bit like asking a fellow to lend you his wife, but do you think I could possibly borrow your gun?"

I had a rather nice twelve bore which I guarded jealously, but I could scarcely say 'No'—and anyway I saw prospects.

"Why yes, Sir, of course."

"Oh good. Jolly decent of you. Look, why don't you come and have a go in one of our aircraft some day."

Prospects were evidently taking shape, so after a decent interval I went apprehensively to his office at the airfield:

"I don't know whether you remember, Sir, but a little while ago you said I might possibly have a go in one of your Hurricanes, and I wonder if that might be possible now?"

"Oh, did I? Yes. Well look, go and see Flight Lieutenant so and so down at dispersal and tell him I sent you."

So I went.

[1]Squadron Leader H G Morison's account of his experiences in obtaining information about German aircraft and armaments, and in spreading disinformation among the enemy, are available on tape in the Sound Archives of the Imperial War Museum.

"Your CO sent me down to say that I could have a go in one of your aircraft and could you please fix me up."

"He said *WHAT*? I suppose you've flown a Hurricane before...? You haven't? Jesus Christ!"

However, despite his understandable concern he found me an aircraft, explained the cockpit layout and sent me off. Not that much explanation was needed. The Hurricane was another Hawker aircraft and its evolution from the Hart was obvious. Everything seemed much the same except for two wings in place of four and a Rolls Royce Merlin with about double the power of the Hart's Rolls Royce Kestrel. It was a little disappointing really, though it was the nearest I ever got to a Spitfire. Anyway, I evidently didn't disgrace myself, because ten days later I was let loose again and this time with Neville, who had managed to get in on the act. The Flight Commander was emphatic: "No aerobatics, no formation flying, no flying over the sea, and behave yourselves," he ordered; but this time I'm afraid we were so pleased with ourselves that on our return we beat up the aerodrome in formation and so were in deep disgrace.

A little later the Hurricanes departed from Elgin, leaving behind one of their aircraft, which was unserviceable. As it was still there a few weeks later it seemed they must have forgotten it, so our engineer officer set about making it go. Eventually the day came when it was pronounced fit to fly and the finger pointed at me as the most experienced Hurricane pilot on the station! By the time all was ready quite a crowd had gathered, expecting me to put on a good show. Slightly apprehensively I climbed into the cockpit, started the engine and warmed it up, then ran it up to full throttle and tested the magnetoes; but as I did so there was a horrendous series of bangs from the exhaust and a drop in revs which should have been enough to have me switch off and send for the fitter. However, the crowd was watching and many of them had laboured to get the aircraft serviceable so I felt I could scarcely disappoint them. Anyway, my pride would not have allowed me to chicken out on the excuse of what the audience would have dismissed as a few meagre little bangs from the exhaust, so I opened the throttle and went.

I had only climbed a few hundred feet when I saw the panel which gives access to the guns on the starboard wing come loose and start to flap about in the slipstream. I expected it to roll the aircraft over and kill me as well, but nothing happened so I flew round cautiously and landed. Once safely down I thought my worries were over for the day. Not a bit of it. The sergeant rigger climbed onto the wing, banged the panel back into place, locked the fasteners with a great big screwdriver and shouted:

"Right you are Mr Morison, Sir. Off you go again."

There was nothing for it, so I took off, flew round for twenty minutes and landed, to everyone's satisfaction. So now we had the luxury of our own private Hurricane, or so we thought, but someone somewhere was doing the paperwork and discovered that he was short of an aircraft, so a few days later our beautiful Hurricane was flown away.

The mess at Blackfriar's Haugh was a convivial place, and it had one unique advantage: the Adjutant was from high society, with a butler whom he had contrived to get not only into the RAF, but also to Elgin as mess sergeant. It was not in every mess that the steward would hold up a glass to the light and polish it before pouring you a drink, but that was the sort of service we enjoyed. As in all messes a great deal of beer was consumed, most of it pretty thin, sour stuff, although the Guinness managed to hold its quality. Much beer was drunk while singing 'The Muffin Man Who Lives In Drury Lane'—that tiresome game where you have to sing the song while balancing a full pint glass on your head—or perhaps we sang 'The Ball of Kirriemuir', the antics at which event are unfortunately unrepeatable. One day, however, the scene in the mess was less convivial. The previous night a car had driven into the river which flowed past our lawn and we gathered on the grass to watch the police hauling it out. As the car emerged from the deep water we could see a body inside which still appeared to be trying to claw its way out. All in the day's work for a policeman maybe—but not for the gallant young airmen and we retreated to the bar, in urgent need of a strong drink.

I must have been something of a trial to our excellent mess sergeant, because I kept bringing in rabbits and hares which I had shot and even in war time you can have too much rabbit. I had got to know a local garage proprietor, George Brown, who used to take me shooting. The moors teemed with hares and in winter there were hare hunts. The hares were unwanted because they ate food which was meant for sheep and so anyone with a gun was welcome. These hunts were quite an adventure; perhaps thirty or forty guns would form a huge circle on the moor and then move in towards the centre, driving the hares before them. As the circle closed in the lads became excited and George's advice was to forget about the hares and keep your head down. It was good advice. On New Year's Day I went shooting with George and his uncle, who was a farmer. The old man did not own the game rights on his farm and so we made a resolution to shoot pheasants only if we were out of sight, but we hadn't gone far before George stopped and, pulling out his hip flask, said: "My its awfu' cauld. I think we'll have a Wee New Year." Well, after that we had Wee New Years at frequent intervals and soon were shooting at anything and everything. We ended up at the farm with an enormous lunch, followed by an enormous tea. After which I felt that I had done enough for the day, but at ten o'clock that night I was trying to instil the finer points of night landings into what seemed to be an unaccountably hopeless pupil.

I had come to know George because he had expertly mended my ancient motor bike. This was a 600cc Douglas, an enormously long beast because its two cylinders were arranged fore and aft. I called it 'Sholto' after Air Marshal Sir William Sholto Douglas, C-in-C Fighter Command, in the hope that this tribute to the gods might induce a posting to Spitfires, but alas it proved ineffective. 'Sholto' had had a predecessor, which was a similar, but smaller twin cylinder Douglas called 'Pollock', after the Able Seaman of that name, because he seldom fired on more than one cylinder. At the beginning of the war 'Pollock' wouldn't go at all and I had perhaps the most nerve racking ride of my life when I got Derek to tow me from Cheam to Cambridge behind his car, in the blackout. Neville Booth had 'Francisco' and I had 'Sholto', but we had difficulty in getting enough fuel. Ordinary motor fuel was severely rationed and the use of aviation fuel was strictly forbidden. However, one night a Wimpey crash-landed on the airfield and ruptured its tanks, from which a small but steady stream of the precious fluid poured out onto the grass. Such waste seemed a shame, so Neville and I found some two gallon cans and managed to fill a couple each. At the time I was billetted out in Lossie and in the dim light of dawn bicycled out carrying the cans of petrol and trying to hide them from the gate sentry, like a naughty schoolboy. 'Sholto' was grateful; he was always at his best on 100 octane.

In December 1941 I was transferred to 'C' Flight, converting pilots onto Wellingtons. They had had basic training on light twin engined aircraft at FTS and were now to fly the real thing. Many had trained in Canada so it would have been weeks, or even months, since they had last flown and often I felt that I was teaching them how to fly from scratch. My initiation as a flying instructor did not, as had once been envisaged, involve a course at the Central Flying School. Instead, on 12 December Polly Parsons took me on a brief flight, pretending to be my pupil, and on the 13th sent me off with my first two real pupils for 3½ hours. It was at night and it was at Lossie, from which I had never flown at night before. Thinking it best to come clean with the first pupil and gain his co-operation, I said: "Well, I've never done this before, but if we both try hard I expect we'll be okay." We were, and I went on to teach pupils nearly every night until the end of the month.

Much of the time we just did circuits and bumps, but that was the most dangerous. On take off the engines were on full power, so if one was going to fail that was the most likely time, and a Wellington had no hope of climbing on one engine. In fact, engine failures were extremely rare. Aircraft had short lives, so most were fairly new and enjoyed devoted attention by the ground crews, even though Neville Booth maintained that the comment most characteristic when you needed something urgently was: "If it's petrol you want, Sir, I'm afraid you've 'ad it. I'm only the electrician and my mate's on early tea."

Things might go wrong on take off, but landings could be exciting too. One night my pupil bounced the aircraft so badly that we ballooned up into the air, almost without flying speed. Usually, a quick blast of full throttle would let us down without breaking anything, but this time when I closed the throttles again a broken linkage left one engine at full bore. A bouncing aircraft without enough flying speed, with one engine on and one off, has a very short expectation of life, but a quick dive across the pupil's lap to switch both off saved a disaster. However, I was stuck in the middle of the flare path with no engines, an astonished pupil and an irate duty officer.

Lossie was a grass field, as was every other station I had been on. At night we had a flare path of a double row of wretched little glim lamps, plus a floodlight to illuminate the moments before landing. Standing by the floodlight at the beginning of the flare path, waiting for aircraft to land, was always a strangely romantic experience. The night sky might be silent. Then from the stillness would come the faint sound of an aircraft, growing louder, then fading again as the pilot throttled back on his final approach. Suddenly the big black shape would materialise out of the darkness. The floodlight would blaze momentarily as it touched down— then blackness again. There was a magic about it, even if it was only an aircraft returning from a training flight, but aircraft on operations also flew from Lossie so it might be one safely back from Norway, or Denmark, or Germany. Then there was relief.

Compared with the little field at Sibson where I had got lost one dark night, Lossie was a vastly confusing place in the blackout. One night a WAAF who was driving a lorry found herself hopelessly lost until she saw two parallel lines of lights stretching into the distance. Obviously they lead somewhere so, no doubt with a sigh of relief, she started to drive along between them, at which moment three unsuspecting people were about to get a shock: the WAAF driver, the officer in charge of the flare path and the pilot of an approaching Wimpey. With the aircraft almost on the ground, the floodlight was switched on and all was revealed. There was a scream from two engines suddenly on full throttle, a great deal of swearing, and a WAAF who must have thought the world was coming to an end, but mercifully it didn't and the aircraft just managed to clear the lorry.

In summer the nights were short. Indeed, if the sky was clear it scarcely got dark at all, so teaching night flying was a problem. Night after night you were up in the small hours, but at least that left the days clear. I had a room at that time in the town and often returned with the sunrise, went for a walk along the deserted beach, had breakfast and then slept till lunch time. Conversely, in winter the nights were very dark and cold, and seemed interminable. For a new pupil, arrived maybe from Canada, with about 150 hours flying and that some months ago, first flights on these dark nights could be traumatic. Instead of a simple little aircraft in peaceful Canada the aircraft was big and black and had guns. The sky was dark, the ground invisible, and it was easy to become disoriented just flying a simple circuit and to make the fatal error of not believing the instruments. One of my pupils found the task so overwhelming that he shook the stick furiously and shouted at the aircraft: "Oh! You bastard!"—at least I hope he was shouting at the aircraft and not at me. He needed coaxing, but got himself and the aircraft back under control and landed safely.

As it was vital never to allow a pupil to become frightened of his aircraft it was necessary to show him that he was the master. I had one pupil who wanted to bale out when the airspeed indicator failed, because he didn't believe it was possible to land safely without one. But by the time we had finished he had learnt that you could. With another pupil we were practicing forced landings and I had closed the throttles.

"Right. Your engines have failed. What are you going to do?"

Blank look.

"Well, there's the airfield down there. If you must crash try and crash on an airfield. They've got fire engines and ambulances."

"I'll never get down. We're far too high."

"Oh yes you will, if you try. Put your wheels down. Put the flaps down. Side slip. Anything to lose height."

"What, side slip a Wellington?"

"Yes, for heaven's sake. Watch."

In fact, the Wellington was a most forgiving aircraft and he had nothing to fear except his inexperience.

Another problem was if a particular aircraft got a bad name. We had one like that, which was reputed to be under-powered and to possess every vice under the sun.

"Oh no, Sir. We're not in V-Victor, are we, Sir?"

"Why not? What's wrong with it?"

"Well, Sir, it's a dreadful aircraft."

"Nonsense. I've never found anything wrong with it. Come on, let's get in and have a go."

Well, maybe it was a little sluggish, but the problem was mainly in his mind.

Most pupils coped well, although there were a few whom we would like to have taken off flying. One in particular was a danger to himself and his crew, not to mention his instructors, but he wasn't English and Allied politics must have been at work, because try as we might we couldn't get rid of him. It was a daunting thought that very soon he would be flying off to Germany on trips of five or six hours, or more, at night and often in foul weather, with people shooting at him.

At Lossie we taught pilots to fly Wellingtons, but nothing about bombing tactics, which was strange, as most of the instructors had operational experience. On reaching a squadron these newcomers would be given only a few trips as second pilot before becoming aircraft captains. Much of the training was realised to be woefully inadequate, so in April 1941, to help get vital lessons across, the Air Ministry introduced a little magazine, 'TEE EMM', which stood for Training Memoranda. It was a monthly booklet written in a chatty style, but very intelligently, and was illustrated by, among others, Fougasse, a distinguished cartoonist of the day. 'TEE EMM' sought to drive its lessons home through the antics of its protagonist, Pilot Officer Prune, a lamentably casual and sloppy officer who committed every possible aeronautical solecism. He suffered from chronic finger trouble (a common complaint in the RAF) and consequently had as his motto: 'Dieu et Mon Doigt' (*sic*) and also another motto: 'Faith et Blind Hope'.

P.O. Prune says—
" We don't want your
navigation."

The sayings of P/O Prune. From 'TEE EMM'.

The introduction to the first issue of 'TEE EMM' is worth reproducing, not least because maybe it still has a message for us today. Also worth reading is an example of some very practical advice for bomber crews which was in the May 1941 issue:

Number 1   April 1941

I hope that these Training Memoranda will be widely read and studied, since I am certain that they will help us all to improve our efficiency, not only in our training but also in operations against the enemy.

C. Portal.

Air Chief Marshal
Chief of the Air Staff

INTRODUCING TEE EMM

THIS is the first issue of a new Air Ministry Publication, a monthly Memorandum on Training. It is perhaps a little different from the usual run of such publications, but new things frequently *are* different. The Royal Air Force, compared with the Navy and the Army, is a new Service. Our traditions are brilliant, but do not yet stretch very far back. But we *have* a tradition of ebullience, even of unconventionality—in short a tradition of the Spirit of Youth and all that Youth implies.

It is not, therefore, out of keeping with this tradition that TEE EMM, the new R.A.F. Training Memorandum, should in a small way reflect this spirit by an occasional intrusion of lightheartedness into serious subjects, by an occasional unconventionality of treatment, by an occasional lack of stiffness in the presentation of training and instructional points and information.

There is no harm in humour ; there is indeed a lot of good. You remember General Wavell's recent story. After the last war the Germans decided that the chief reason why they had failed to win was the British staying power, which they attributed largely to the British sense of humour. They determined, therefore, with Teutonic thoroughness, to inculcate humour in their own armies—with a view no doubt of making certain of the next war. To this end they included in their military manual an order that humour was to be cultivated, and added an appendix containing different types of English jokes for their soldiers to study. One illustration showed Bruce Bairnsfather's famous picture of Old Bill, sitting morosely in a building with an enormous hole blown through it, while young 'Bert, a newcomer to the trenches, is asking " What made that 'ole ? " Old Bill's grumpy answer is, " Mice ! " To this the German editor had appended a solemn footnote of explanation : " It was not mice really ; it was a shell ! "

If you think over that story you will see why we have, in TEE EMM, tried to avoid too heavy a touch. For the British do not need *too* heavy an emphasising and explaining of the seriousness of this war and of the part each man has to play in it. They are capable of talking about " mice " but realising the " shell-fire "—without having the joke explained. It is because they are capable of this that their mentality is different from that of the Germans. And it is because of this different mentality that they won the last war and will win this.

The occasional joke, the occasional use of " unofficial " language, the occasional avoidance of " Whitehallese " never hurt anyone yet—and probably does a power of good. For just as underneath the outward light-heartedness of the officers and men of the Royal Air Force of to-day there is the constant realisation of the grim purpose every one of them has before him, so too will they realise that TEE EMM in whatever form it is written, contains serious matter, the whole object of which is to *help*. The stuff, in short, is there.

WHAT THE HUN IS DOING

II

CO-OPERATION between Hun night-fighters and ground defences is frequently very good. A short while ago one of our bombers flying over Holland at 10,000 feet was suddenly ringed round by red flares shot up from the ground. Wisely the pilot changed course abruptly—just in time to avoid by 150 yards a German night-fighter which was swooping down on this red target circle to see what he could find in the bull's-eye.

White and yellow circles round fuselage markings have recently resulted in Hun planes being mistaken for friendly aircraft.

The Hun is still playing games with his navigation lights in night operations. Recently an E.A. picked up by searchlights, retired hastily in one direction—and promptly reappeared from another, burning navigation lights and trying to look like the other fellows.

It is sometimes inadvisable to assume that an E.A. diving to the sea after a crew of three have baled out has not still got a sting in its tail. A Hurricane approached one such to about thirty yards, in order to watch it pancake. Instead, he got a short sharp burst from the German pilot—luckily with not much damage.

More German searchlight tricks. Searchlights along both sides of a bomber's route raise their beams to 45° to show the track. And searchlights are laid along the ground in the direction the bomber is heading, being raised to the vertical as it passes overhead.

The Hun has been adding to his collection of " decoy ducks " in Germany and occupied countries. Besides the usual dummy aerodromes, flare paths and fires, he is also using lines of flickering lights to look like a stick of incendiaries, often with a grand decoy blaze in the middle of them, and even fake explosions to give " verisimilitude to an otherwise bald and unconvincing " imitation fire.

Finally from 'TEE EMM', an example of 18th Century science fiction:

AN 18th CENTURY PROPHECY

The time will come, when thou shalt lift thine eyes
To watch a long-drawn battle in the skies,
While aged peasants, too amazed for words,
Stare at the flying fleets of wond'rous birds.
England, so long mistress of the sea,
Where winds and waves confess her sovereignty,
Her ancient triumphs yet on high shall bear,
And reign, the sovereign of the conquered air.

(*Translated from Gray's " Luna Habitabilis," Cambridge* 1797.)

At Lossie we were a mixed community. Instructors who had survived a tour of operations, instructors like me who had never seen a gun fired in anger, pupils who would soon be going on operations, and none of us with any worthwhile expectation of survival. We didn't think much about it. One's mind tended to close itself to the prospect of being killed, unless fear emerged from the subconscious and you lost your nerve. It rarely happened, but when it did it it was sad to see. Many were killed or made prisoner before the strain overwhelmed them. We didn't think much, if at all, about the rights and wrongs of war. Anyone who had seen the cones of searchlights, the flicker of bursting flak over the Ruhr and burning aircraft falling out of the sky—or indeed anyone who had yet to see them—just knew that bombing was a job which he had to do. There was little hate against the Germans and certainly we were never taught to hate them. Something was known of Nazi atrocities, because there were neutral journalists and diplomats in Germany, including Americans until Hitler declared war on the United States in December 1941, but these atrocities had relatively little attention in the British press and precious little from us. Our thinking was in simple black and white: there was an enemy; if he could he would invade and kill us, and if he got hurt when we hit back that was his bad luck. We didn't have a very agreeable job to do and we didn't have time for the philosophical thoughts which now come more easily from the comfort of an armchair.

By May 1942, Derek, who never became an engineer officer after all, was a pilot in a Hampden squadron. I went to visit him while on leave and he suggested I should go with him on a night trip to drop mines in the sea near Brest (a job known as 'Gardening'). I remembered what had happened to Neville Booth when he went on a joyride over Denmark, but a trip round the Brittany coast, where there couldn't be many people with guns, seemed quite inviting. However, luckily or not, the weather closed in and the operation was cancelled. Derek had sailed through FTS and OTU and was now half way through his first tour of bomber operations in which he seemed happy enough, but I was more anxious than ever to get out of Bomber Command. Naming my bike after the C-in C-Fighter Command hadn't worked and I was devoid of ideas until one day I heard of something, which probably I shouldn't have heard. It was about 161 Squadron, the unit of the RAF whose job it was to fly people in and out of enemy territory, and this seemed the ideal job for me. They used Lysanders so as to get into small fields—and wasn't I a dab hand with a Lizzie? and wasn't I a dab hand at pilot navigation? and didn't I want a job where I would be an individual, dependent for survival on my own skill and wits? Yes, yes and yes, this was the job for me. So I sat down to compose an application for transfer, which I was convinced would be accepted on account of my obvious suitability.

But alas, as I was sitting in the mess composing it, in walked my CO.

"Good news, Morison, I've got a posting for you at last."

"Oh yes, Sir?"—trying to look keen. "Where to?"

"103 Squadron. They're at Elsham Wolds. They've got Wellingtons, but they're converting to Halifaxes—and by the way, you're promoted to Flight Lieutenant."

So there it was. There was nothing I could do about it now, so I sent a telegram to my parents which said simply: "With the compliments of Flight Lieutenant Morison." Then, on 25 May 1942, an Anson flew me and an enormous load of my kit to Aberdeen, where I boarded the train for Lincolnshire.

CHAPTER FOUR

By Air to Germany

'I like to fly to Germany
And watch them chuck up flak at me,
Then paddle back across the sea.
It's foolish but it's fun.'

Elsham Wolds

RAF Elsham Wolds was about ten miles south of the Humber, near the small country town of Brigg, and was one of the rash of wartime airfields which were built all over the flat lands of East Anglia, Lincolnshire and Yorkshire to be as near as possible to the principal targets in Germany. There were wooden buildings, a long concrete runway, not a lot else.

So there I was, second in command of 'A' Flight in a squadron which, unlike 241 at Inverness, was engaged night after night with the enemy. I arrived just after breakfast following a gruesome night train journey from Scotland, and there can have been no time to waste, for the same morning I was in the air in a brand new Wellington called 'British Guiana II'. I was getting acquainted with the locality and, most importantly, with my crew. All of them had extensive operational experience, while not only was mine nil, but, like the pupils at OTU, no one had ever taught me anything about how to survive a trip over Germany. However, I did bring with me the best bit of advice any bomber pilot could have had, and it came from Derek when he heard that I was posted to a squadron: 'Whatever you do Wally, weave—weave like the clappers!" To 'weave' was to fly an irregular course so as to confuse the flak and the night fighters. Derek had another recipe for survival which he called 'The Inverse Met Law', which meant that you always assumed the weather would be the opposite of what was forecast. He claimed that it was infallible, and evidently he had conscientiously followed his own advice because he had just completed his first thirty-trip tour of operations without mishap.

My Flight Commander was S/Ldr Godfrey, and he took on the job of showing me the ropes. First of all he seemed to think it neccessary to make sure that I could fly a Wellington properly, but after all those countless circuits and bumps there wasn't much doubt about that. As we landed after a local flight his comment was: "Oh, very professional." But I would need more than that to get myself safely to the Ruhr and back.

Three nights after I had arrived Godfrey took me as second pilot and we set out for Paris to attack the Gnome & Rhône aero-engine works at Gennevilliers, which is on the Seine just to the north west of the city. The need was to destroy the factory, but with the least damage to Paris, so it had to be a precision attack at low level and on a clear moonlit night. Most bombing operations were carried out roughly between 10,000 and 20,000 feet. Wellingtons and Stirlings couldn't manage much more than 15,000, Lancasters 20,000 and Mosquitoes 30,000 (Oh! for a Mosquito). On this trip we flew at about 6000 feet, and as we crossed the French coast and headed for Paris the countryside below looked peaceful in the moonlight. Indeed, all was uneventful until we approached the target. Paris was not heavily defended, but we were low enough to be in range of the light flak[1] and ahead we could see a lot of tracer flying about the sky.

Being on the river the target was easy to locate—at least the immediate vicinity was easy, but to distinguish the actual buildings was less so. Anyway, we dropped our load of two 1000 lb bombs, plus two five hundreds and one two hundred and fifty pounder. As soon as the bombs had gone it seemed to me to be time to go home while the going was good, but not so Godfrey. He now gave me what I thought was a quite unnecessary display of *sang froid*. As the tracer floated up towards us (tracer does appear to float slowly up until it gets near, when it zips past, or at least you hope it does) he turned away from the target and circled round with Paris spread out below in the moonlight.

"Do you know Paris at all, Morison? Beautiful city. Look, down there's the Arc de Triomphe and over there's the Eiffel Tower."

---

[1]'Flak': a contraction of the German *Flugzeugabwehrkanone*, or 'Aircraft Defence Cannon'.

Well yes, it was a beautiful sight, but this scarcely seemed the time for a Cook's Tour. But it was a good lesson in keeping calm over the target, and soon we headed back across the still peaceful countryside. Peaceful it may have looked, but that did not mean that the sky was a friendly place, so we kept a sharp lookout for fighters until well out over the sea.

Although a huge effort had been put into the bomber offensive, the results had been disappointing because of difficulty in locating targets accurately except from low altitude and in perfect weather. Such conditions, of course, also favoured the defence, so that only lightly defended, or very important targets, could be attacked in that way. Air Marshal Sir Arthur Harris, C-in-C Bomber Command, had oversold his ability to bring Germany to her knees by bombing and he badly needed a spectacular success to restore his personal prestige, as well as that of his Command. Accordingly he resolved to assemble a force of 1000 aircraft to attack either Hamburg or Cologne. Both were major cities and would be easy to locate in clear weather, Cologne being on the Rhine and Hamburg at the head of the Elbe estuary. He believed that such a large force, if concentrated in a short time over the target, would saturate the defences and that therefore it would be an acceptable risk to go on a clear moonlit night. A force of two or three hundred bombers was more usual, and to assemble as many as a thousand meant that not only had every posible front line aircraft to be included, but that it would be necessary to press into service aircraft from OTUs, manned by both instructors and pupils.

The night after our trip to Paris the first 'Thousand Bomber Raid' was on, but because of bad weather over Hamburg it was to Cologne. Again I went with Godfrey, and although flying over heavily defended Holland and Germany was not like a jaunt to Paris the theory about saturating the defences worked. We saw no fighters, and no flak or searchlights came near us, though as we approached the target in brilliant moonlight I could see the sky teeming with friendly aircraft, above, below and on either side. My log book says there were 1200, but in fact the total which finally took off was 1046. Harris had been advised that statistically only one collision should be expected among this swarm of aircraft closely packed together in the night sky and that was what happened. All of us headed towards a fantastic scene of searchlights, the flicker of bursting flak, fires on the ground and the Rhine reflecting the moonlight. As we flew nearer I could see the city clearly, and everywhere there were great patches of fire.

We were carrying incendiaries and I was acting as bomb aimer. Our aiming point was already a sea of flame, so I aimed our load near to the edge of it. This time Godfrey turned straight for home and I went into the astrodome to watch for fighters.

We reached home with the dawn and learned that of the twenty aircraft which went from Elsham one was missing, one was damaged by a night fighter, which killed the second pilot, and one crashed on landing, killing several of the crew. In all forty aircraft were lost, so evidently some squadrons were more fortunate than us, but forty out of 1046 is less than four per cent, which was an unusually low loss.

Although the raid was nothing compared with what was to come in 1943 and 1944, the destruction was enormous: 469 people killed, 45,000 homeless, 13,000 houses and 106 factories destroyed or severely damaged; but all we knew as we headed for home was that Cologne appeared to be ablaze from end to end and that the defences were largely paralysed.

Next morning *The Times* had headlines: "Over a thousand bombers raid Cologne. Biggest air attack of the war. 2000 tons of bombs dropped in forty minutes." On the other side *The Volkischer Beobachter*, the Nazi Party's popular daily paper, said that it was a '*Terrorangriff*' and that forty four British aircraft were destroyed, both of which statements were near enough true. Churchill telegraphed to Roosevelt: "I hope you were pleased with our mass air attack on Cologne. There is plenty more to come." There was indeed.

Watching for night fighters meant staring into the darkness hour after hour, trying to concentrate and knowing that if you relaxed for a moment it might be then that a fighter would open fire. If you didn't see him first the chances of survival were negligible and even if you did they were none too good. Pity the poor tail gunner whose lot it was to keep watch throughout the trip and who was in the most exposed position if the shooting started. Some people doubted the value of carrying gun turrets, whose weight and shape slowed the aircraft and required two extra crew to be carried, and they were proved right when the Mosquito came into service.

It needed only two crew and when used as a bomber carried no armament. It relied on its speed, which was the equal of a German night fighter, and it could fly high enough to be virtually out of range of flak.

Having scraped to the very bottom of the barrel to assemble his thousand bomber force Harris wanted to use it again before it had to be dispersed. Two nights later, on 1 June 1942, it headed for Essen, the great industrial city in the Ruhr valley. Again I flew with Godfrey, but half way across the North Sea the wireless operator reported that he had received a 'BBA', the code transmitted in Morse which ordered 'Return to base'. Godfrey was doubtful. The weather was good and there was no apparent reason for such an order. He questioned the wireles operator at length, for you could quickly get a bad reputation if you turned back on some lame excuse, and it would look particularly bad for a flight commander. But the W/Op remained adamant that he had received the 'BBA'. We couldn't check because we had to maintain radio silence and so there was nothing for it but turn back. Being a more or less surplus member of the crew meant that I didn't have much to do except think how unpleasant it would be over the Ruhr and I can't say that I was sorry to be heading for Lincolnshire.

Once instructions for a raid had been received from Bomber Command the preparation was a formal affair, starting with a written order from the station commander to the squadron commander which set out: (i) the target and any alternative targets—the final alternative sometimes being 'any built up area in Germany'; (ii) the purpose of the attack, for example 'to cause maximum damage'; and (iii) the number of aircraft, with the names of the crews and the bomb and petrol loads for each aircraft. The aircrews got their instructions at briefing where it was all set out on large maps showing the target, the latest information on flak, searchlights, fighters, the weather and the suggested route. Briefings could be pretty tense affairs.

The night after the abortive Essen trip we went to Dieppe, but now I was the captain. The Channel ports were the nursery slopes, being lightly defended, easy to find and involving the minimum of flying over enemy territory. We carried fourteen 250 lb bombs and dropped them on the docks from 10,000 feet. On our first run over the target we dropped half the load. Then we came round for a second run

From:-   Officer Commanding, R.A.F. Station, Elsham Wolds.

To:-   Officer Commanding No.103 Squadron, R.A.F.Station, Elsham Wolds.(2 copies)
         1 Copy for File.

Date:-   2nd. June, 1942.

Ref:-   Form 'B', Serial No. 696.

EXECUTIVE ORDERS FOR OPERATIONS 2/3rd, June,1942.

4 Aircraft from No. 103 Squadron.

Intention:- To destroy DOCKS and SHIPPING.

Target: Primary:-   DIEPPE DOCKS.

         Alternative:- NIL.

         Last Resort:- NIL.

Route Out: Base---5 miles S. of Spilsby---5 miles S.W. of Newbury---Worthing---
                                                   ---Target.

Route Home: Reverse of above.

Bomb and Petrol Load.

A/C	Captain.	Bomb Load.			Petrol.
N	F/L. Morrison.	14 x 250 lb.	G.P.T.D.	0.025.	634 gallons.
K	Sgt. Tew.	"	"	"	"
R	Sgt. Vickary.	"	"	"	"
W	Sgt. Smith.	"	"	"	"

Signals Procedure: No.1 Group, Signals Instructions No. 8.

Photographs: All aircraft to carry cameras.

Order of Take-Off: First aircraft "N" at 0038 hours.
                     Remainder in above order at 2 minute intervals.

Reconnaissance: Results of own and previous sorties.

Briefing: 1930 hours.

Nickels: 10 Bundles per aircraft to fall on AMIENS district.

                                            Evans 8/br.

                               Group Captain, Commanding,
                               R.A.F. Station, Elsham Wolds, Lincs.

Official order for the attack on Dieppe docks, 2 June 1942.

and all was well until I put my hand out to open the bomb doors and accidentally switched on the landing lights. It was a boob of which P/O Prune would have been justly proud, and it was nearly the end of us as every flak gunner in Dieppe latched on to this beautifully illuminated target. As soon as the bombs were gone we turned for home, but the tracer came floating up, perilously close, while the tail gunner called out directions to keep us clear:

"Dive skipper! Dive like shit! Turn left...Turn right. Dive!"

We streaked out to sea as fast as a Wellington knew how until we were out of range and could get our breath back. Then we settled down to the long haul back to Lincolnshire. (I can't have been the only person stupid enough to make the mistake of switching on the landing lights, as the switch was perilously near the bomb release; later Wellingtons had a guard over the light switch.)

It was a fine clear night so navigation was no problem, but I thought I would try out a new radio position-finding system which was supposed to be in operation. Our main wireless communication was by morse code, which had long range, but meant that we had to carry a wireless operator. However, the pilot had a radio telephone set, which had only very short range and was used mainly for talking to the control tower when near the airfield. Because of the short range the idea was to put out a call so that if any RAF station heard you it was unlikely to be more than ten miles away, and by replying and identifying itself it could give you an approximate position. This would be very much a poor man's position-finding system, but after a long trip over Germany with never a sight of the ground a returning aircraft could be as much as a hundred miles off course. If the system worked, it would be a great deal better than nothing. But would it work? I thought the time had come to find out. You had to transmit a code word and the word was 'Darky':

"Hallo Darky, Hallo Darky, Hallo Darky."

Silence ensued, so I tried again. More silence. You can feel very stupid flying along and calling 'Darky' to an unresponsive night sky, so I gave up. (Whether anyone ever got a position out of 'Darky' I don't know, but I doubt it. Indeed, I never met anyone else who had even heard of it so maybe the whole thing was some sort of practical joke.) 'Darky' had failed us so we resumed more conventional navigation and arrived safely at Elsham as the sun rose.

A couple of nights later it was Essen. This was it. No more nursery slopes. This was serious stuff. The Ruhr. The very heart of Germany's armaments industry. Coal, steel, the Krupp works, the lot. For this reason it was known, un-lovingly, to bomber crews as 'The Happy Valley'. Amazing as it may seem, I was so naive that I did not know that the original Happy Valley, where fornication rather than flak was the vogue, was in Kenya.

After briefing we had some time to spare, so I went to the parachute section to change my parachute. There were two sorts. One, which you sat on, was for pilots, who mainly stayed put in their seats, but if you had to move about that sort was too constricting. The other type had the canopy sep-arate from the harness and you clipped it to hooks on your chest if you needed it. The Wellington pilot's seat had the recess for a seat type and that was what I took, comforted by the thought that, being permanently attached, it was im-mediately ready for use. After that I wandered back to the flight office and went over the route with our navigator. Then it was time to go.

Out to dispersal in a truck and climb on board. I had done the usual night flying test flight earlier in the day, with the rest of the crew, but now we checked everything again. Engines started, warmed up, run up to full throttle and the magnetoes tested. No mag drops this time as there had been with the Elgin Hurricane; everything was in perfect order. One after another the squadron aircraft started to roll along the perimeter track towards the end of the runway and we took our place in the queue, a nasty hollow feeling in the stomach. We reached the runway and after a pause got the signal to go. With the engines at full throttle, a chorus of "Good luck, Skipper," came from the crew over the intercom. Good luck was certainly something we all needed. Just airborne by the end of the runway. Wheels up. Flaps up. Head for Mablethorpe on the coast. Slowly we climbed across the North Sea, feeling happier now that we were on our way.

We crossed the enemy coast at the ominously named Dutch island of Overflakkee, and from 14,000 feet could see far ahead towards the Ruhr cones of searchlights, the flicker of bursting flak and the glow of fires. Soon a mass of flares burst into light in the sky. They had to be marking Essen, and after a quick check with the navigator I altered course a few degrees to port. We were headed for an inferno, but for the moment all was quiet. Then suddenly:

"Aircraft to port, Skipper!"

The intercom call was urgent, but it was already too late; the dark shape of another Wellington flashed in front of us and we hit, not head on, but probably with our starboard wing. Instantly we went out of control, heading for the ground in a spiral dive. There was just blackness, howling wind and my two shouted words:

"Abandon Aircraft!"

But what chance was there? The tail gunner might be okay. He could swing his turret round to the beam and fall out backwards. But for the navigator and wireless operator the outlook was bleak. In an aircraft standing on its nose and wildly lurching round they would have to find their parachute packs, hook them on and struggle to a hatch in the cockpit. But I was lucky; there was an escape hatch right above my head. I pulled it open, undid my harness and struggled up against the slipstream; then suddenly it plucked me out and everything went black.

I was falling free and there was maybe a minute before I would hit the ground. I had banged my head on something, probably the tail fin, and only slowly came to my senses. When I did it was like one of those dreams in which you try to run, but can only crawl. I knew there was something I had to do and I knew that it was urgent. Yes, that's it; I had to pull the rip-cord. I set about the task so painfully slowly and deliberately that it seemed I might be too late, but at last I found it and pulled. Nothing happened and I had a moment's despair until the parachute opened with a bang and I was floating silently down, right way up now, through the summer night sky. Everything became gentle and peaceful, but not for long. Seconds later I was crashing through hedgerow trees. The canopy caught in the branches and left me hanging, but fortunately only just above the ground, so I banged the quick release and stepped onto German soil.

And so, to adapt Eliot a little:

> 'The 'chute in a tree suspended
> Marked the place where the story ended.'

Marked it, anyway, as far as flying was concerned.

R.A.F. Form 540

21703 Wt. 38805/3593 400.000 12/39 WIC 4 Co-51-5658

See instructions for use of this form in K.R. and A.C.I.,
para. 2349, and War Manual, Pt. II., chapter XX., and
notes in R.A.F. Pocket Book.

OPERATIONS RECORD BOOK

Page No. 3.

No. of pages used for day

of (Unit or Formation) No. 103 Squadron, RAF Elsham Wolds, Lincs.

Place	Date	Time	Summary of Events	References to Appendices
E S S E N. (Cont'd.)				
			E S S E N. (Cont'd.)	
	5.6.42. to 6.6.42.	22.51 to 04.54.	Visibility was good apart from a slight ground haze and moderate flak was encountered over the target. From between 10,000 and 14,000 feet bombs were dropped and successful results were seen.	
			P/O. Gosman abandoned the mission when 10 miles North of DAUDEN owing to the starboard engine over-heating and returned to base with all bombs. F/Lt. Morison did not return and the following have therefore been posted to No. 1 R.A.F. Depot, non-effective missing:- 884,76 F/Lt. W.McD.Morison, 976873 Sgt. Traquair, W.L., 1154055 Sgt. Walters, E.D., 1101856 Sgt. Grieve, R.E.P., 749430 F/Sgt. Coxon, J.H.	
			All other aircraft returned safely.	

The squadron Operations Record Book recorded simply: "Flight Lieutenant Morison did not return."

To Dulag Luft by way of Düsseldorf

It was traumatic. One moment I was high in the sky, free and in command. I had power at my fingertips and even a reasonable expectation of breakfast in the mess. The next moment I was standing in a German hayfield, immobilised, listening enviously to the sound of homeward bound aircraft and facing the imminent prospect of becoming a prisoner, or worse. I took stock of my situation. I found that my left arm was useless and my head was bleeding. I felt dopey and had lost my flying boots. Perhaps the best thing to do was to lie down and think things over. That didn't help, so I started to get up again, but a searing pain in my shoulder stopped me. If I couldn't move it was inevitable that I would become a prisoner, and I thought: well, maybe the sooner the better, so I blew my whistle and even shouted, but it was as silly and ineffective as calling 'Darky'. Then I heard dogs barking and pistol shots, and decided that if that was the reception one of my crew was getting perhaps I had better shut up. So there I lay until with the daylight there came a peasant driving a horse and cart and with him a little girl. I could just have been in Holland, but no such luck:

"Are you German?" I asked.

"Yes. Did you drop by parachute?"

"Yes."

"Are you wounded?"

"Yes."

With that he sent the girl for help and calmly proceeded to scythe his grass until soon two policemen arrived.

"Get up," they said.

"I can't."

They pointed guns at me. I got up, all pain forgotten. Guns can be great pain killers.

I was now a Prisoner of War—a *Kriegsgefangener*, a 'Kriegie'—but standing groggily in that early morning hay field I had precious little idea what to expect.

The status of prisoners was defined in "The Geneva Convention of 27 July 1929 Relative to the Treatment of Prisoners of War" of which both Britain and Germany were signatories. It covered every aspect in meticulous, and often unrealistic, detail—as can be seen from the few extracts in Appendix A. But it boiled down to an obligation to treat prisoners decently. In practice, the regular forces of the *Wehrmacht* (the Army, the *Luftwaffe* and the *Kriegsmarine*) observed the Convention, at least in its essentials, but only as regards the British and Americans—ie, the Aryans. If you were a Russian or a Pole you were unlikely to be so lucky because Slavs were regarded in the Nazi demonology as an inferior race and not much better than Jews, who were officially classed as sub-human. The SS and the Gestapo did not care about the Convention and they were the ones who wrought havoc wherever the Nazi writ ran. Early Kriegies had established their rights by courageously insisting: "I am a British Officer and I demand —." This formula could even work with the Gestapo, as they expected their prisoners to cringe and were thrown off balance if they did not. But just then none of this was in my mind. I did not know what to expect and was wary, but bewildered.

The countryside where I had come down was peaceful and untouched by war, and as they walked me to a car one of the policemen declared, with an expansive gesture: *"Deutschland nicht kaputt!"*, with which I could not really argue. They took me to a civilian hospital in the little country town of Geldern where I was put in a room with some French prisoners. In broken English they warned me that the doctors would probably cut off my arms and legs if I let them anaesthetise me, and although that hardly seemed likely it was reassuring when an old nun came to take me to X-Ray. After that I was searched and everything was taken away except, amazingly, my tin of escape kit and my wallet of continental money.

An hour or so after arriving I was moved to an operating theatre and on the way passed a legless patient, which seemed to lend some weight to the Frenchmen's warning, but by then I was past caring, and anyway these just seemed to be ordinary kindly people, as indeed they were. In the theatre the young nurse ran her fingers through my tangled, blood-caked hair and murmured *"Schön, nicht wahr? Sind sie verheiratet?*—Lovely isn't it? Are you married?" But this was no moment for dalliance. The anaesthetist, with some tact perhaps, produced a large syringe and said *"Schlaf,"* with appropriate dumb show, then jabbed in the needle and I lapsed into unconsciousness.

When I came to in the room of the pessimistic Frenchmen I still had all my limbs, but also a lot of pain, and I made a fuss until they gave me something to ease it. Then, to my surprise, I was told to get up and dress in order to leave for Düsseldorf. It seemed a bit rough, but Kriegies could not be choosers. It was a very hot day. We walked to the station, and the train journey lasted about three hours. We waited for a connection at Krefeld. We stood in the sweltering heat of Düsseldorf waiting for a tram, then travelled standing for several miles to the suburb of Gerresheim, where I arrived only just able to stand. Hazily, and for the first time, I saw the inside of a prison camp. It was Stalag VIJ, a hospital run by French prisoners for French prisoners.

The French doctor was delighted to see me. He had, he said, another RAF officer in the hospital, and a few minutes later I was uttering a some incoherent words to P/O M N Aicken from New Zealand. I was put to bed and remember nothing more of that day except being held up to write a letter home. I still have this letter, but it is odd. It is addressed in a wobbly hand, but contains no message; and yet there must have been one because my father made a copy of it, which reads:

Dear Pop
All well except broken arm. Being looked after O.K. Inform Air Ministry. Will give address when out of hospital.

It was written on one of the usual prisoners' letter forms, which, quaintly, were marked: 'Post Free. By Airmail.' But all the same it took five weeks to arrive.

Stalag VIJ was not quite what one was used to in a hospital. Pans of noodles and pans of forceps boiled side by side on the stove, while sick Russians sat forlornly in the passages, seemingly just waiting to die and unnoticed by the nursing orderly who, until recently, had been a farm labourer in the Haute Savoie. What was I doing here anyway? It all seemed unreal. A few days ago I had been trying to kill Germans, but now they had patched me up and pointed me along the road to health, even if it was a rough road. And the Russians? Evidently no one cared if they died. It was a crazy world, but since there was no choice I accepted it as normal.

Being both British, and officers, P/O Aicken and I were specially favoured and were given a room with only one other occupant, a Frenchman whom we called Joe, because, I'm afraid, we used to sing 'Poor old Joe, he ain't what he used to be'. Joe had a broken thigh and was destined to lie for two months on a mattress stuffed with wood shavings, his broken leg firmly fixed to a great framework. From his knee a rope ran over a pulley at the end of the bed and from it hung a weight. This may be usual practice in order to keep the broken bone under tension, but what was unusual was that the weight was a large tin full of sand and with a label indicating its original contents. It read: *'Kunstmarmelade. Nur für Kriegsgefangener.'* ('Artificial jam. Only for Prisoners of War'). We were beginning to learn that we were in a different class from ordinary people.

Not only the doctor, but everyone else, liked to show off his medical knowledge and importance by fiddling with Poor old Joe's, leg and as they twisted it to and fro, or made adjustments to the mechanism, Joe would writhe with pain and groan:

"Aooow! Ça me fait du mal."

But the only comfort he ever got was: *"Soyez brave mon vieux. C'est nécessaire."*

Joe looked ill and made gruesome noises when he ate, so it is not surprising that we sang our song, but one day he asked us what this song was about. This was embarrassing, so I explained that it was an old English folk song about a grey mare and after that we thought it best to give it up.

When they learned that I could speak some French a constant stream of visitors turned up, seeking information of every sort. What did I think of Petain? What did the English think of the French armistice? What was the political situation in Russia? Did the bombers know that there was a camp here? (Good question). Did I not think that *"La France a été trahie*—that France had been betrayed?" Most of these questions would have required care and tact to answer in English, let alone in my none too fluent French, but somehow I got by. It occupied the time, but too many visitors in hospital can be a trial at the best of times. History does not relate whether the bombers knew there was a camp at Gerresheim. There were no raids on Düsseldorf while I was there, but there was one a little later and once again fate was at work up there when a Wellington met a German night fighter and another RAF pilot took the first steps towards joining in this story.

The doctors did what they could for us all, but it was not a
lot. The food supplied by the Germans was negligible and
the French lived mainly on parcels sent from home. Medical
supplies were few and the X-Ray was unserviceable. The
doctor said he would try and get some Red Cross food
parcels for us from a depot in the town, but for several days
nothing appeared and I began to wonder if we would ever
gather any strength on a diet of a little bread and margarine,
about half a cubic inch of sausage and some watery porridge.
At least the bread was white, which was a rarity for Kriegies,
but after a few days we were evidently not thought ill enough
for even that diet and instead got an inedible soup, with army
bread. This bread was something which in time Kriegies
came to welcome, but at first most of mine went to the
Russians. They were probably those who, on arrival from the
Eastern front, were too weak to work. They looked starved
and helpless, and were so demoralised that they would
shamble to their feet every time a German soldier passed.

We got a few biscuits from the French Red Cross, but were
starving hungry until a week later one Red Cross parcel
arrived for us. Feeling just about strong enough, I tottered
down to the parcels office to collect it. Probably no child
ever turned over the treasures in its Christmas stocking with
more excitement than a new Kriegie opening his first parcel.
Even veterans could sometimes be seen pulling out tins and
exclaiming:

"Oh great: a tin of bacon!—*Two* bars of chocolate!—
Cheese!—Ah, these wizard biscuits!—What's this: tea or
coffee? Oh, coffee; we'll try and swap that for cocoa. Now
let's see—we'll have this meat roll for lunch..."—and so it
would go on, for food, women and escaping made up most of
the Kriegies' conversation.

The Red Cross parcels were the prisoners' lifeline. In
principle we got one a week, which was fine, but even one
every two weeks was not bad. One every two weeks was
known as 'half parcels'. Most parcels came from Britain,
with some from Canada, New Zealand and other countries
where food was plentiful. By some miracle they found their
way to the Red Cross in Switzerland and then the Germans
took over the transport. The food provided by the Germans
was mainly bread, potatoes and root vegetables, which, so
long as we got the parcels, gave a reasonable diet.

Later we learned that one of Aicken's crew in another

camp had managed to find out where his skipper was and had got the Senior British Officer there to persuade the Germans to send him parcels. More arrived later so our food problems ceased, but we had had our first taste of hunger. Even if it was only a little one it felt bad enough to someone who had never gone hungry before.

Aicken had a dislocated knee. He was frantically impatient to walk again and was convinced that the doctors were being too slow. He had been shot down on the second Thousand Bomber Raid, on Essen, while he was still at OTU. He had come all the way from New Zealand and his flying career had ended before it had really started. He used to curse out loud:

"My God. Why was I such a fool? If only I could get back. I must have another shot. My God I must get back."

Fresh in his mind was advice on ways of escape which he had heard in a lecture by Squadron Leader John Shore, one of the first RAF officers to escape and get back to England. Now that we had some food and felt a bit stronger we thought more and more about escaping. Little as we knew about the business we could see that the camp was only thinly guarded and there were plenty of places where it would have been easy to get through the wire. There were only three sentries for five hundred yards of perimeter, but our physical disabilities kept us in more effectively than barbed wire. All the same we schemed and planned and daydreamed, with ideas which ranged from drifting down the Rhine in a boat to another, which in those days was just a dreamy fantasy: to steal an aeroplane and fly away home.

I still felt very weak. I was told that my shoulder had been dislocated and I had certainly had a bang on the head, both probably from hitting the tail of the aircraft. I had been dragged out of hospital within an hour of a general anaesthetic and had been half starved for a week, but perhaps the real answer came a fortnight later. The doctor sat me on a stool in the operating theatre cum surgery and unwound the chrysalis of cotton wool and bandages which had bound my arm across my chest. He revealed a smell of decomposition and a very depressing sight, for the shoulder and upper arm were coloured a sickly green and the muscles were wasted to nearly nothing. There was virtually no movement in the shoulder or elbow, although my forearm and hand were working. Muttering exclamations of distress and imprecations against the Germans, who he said would shoot him if they saw the amount of bandage he was using, he bound it all up again and there it stayed for a long time, quietly rotting away.

The Germans took little interest in us except that once a day one would peer round the door to make sure we were still there and would utter the words: *"Ja. Tommy."* We hoped this lack of interest would continue until we were well enough to have a serious chance of getting out, but three weeks after my arrival we were told that we were to be moved. I explained to the French doctor that we were anxious to stay and he agreed to do what he could. He expected we would be examined by a German doctor before going, so next morning my temperature recorded a serious rise and my throat was painted an alarming hue. Clearly I was very sick, but it was all to no avail. The German doctor never came and we were peremptorily ordered to be ready at 7am for the journey to *Dulag Luft*, which was short for *Durchgangslager der Luftwaffe*, or Luftwaffe Transit Camp. The Germans liked such contractions and had produced *Stalag* from *Stammlager*, ie, Main Camp; *Oflag* from *Offizierlager*, or Officers' Camp; then there was *Sonderlager* (Special Camp), and in the minds of many prisoners there was lurking somewhere a *Straflager* (Punishment Camp), although in fact no such thing existed, at least within the control of the Wehrmacht.

Dulag was in the small town of Oberursel near Frankfurt on Main and was where all prisoners of the Luftwaffe were taken for interrogation.

When we left, in the charge of an army corporal, it was a relief to be outside the wire again, but it brought home the painful distinction between the prisoner and the free. Not only painful, but somehow unreal, for it was difficult to grasp the difference between us and these people in the street going about their ordinary lives. The only thing apparently separating us was this rather harmless looking corporal, who even left us standing alone on the station platform for several minutes while he searched for our reserved compartment on the Essen to Munich express. Why didn't we slip quietly away? Lack of gumption maybe, but where would we have gone? Two young men in RAF uniform, one hobbling on a broken knee and one with his arm in a sling, would scarcely have got far. In one of the occupied countries it would have been different, but in the heart of Germany the chances were nil.   On board the train we enjoyed a compartment to ourselves, and although it was only a third class one, with wooden seats, we did well, for the corridors were packed with people standing.   Our corporal, who wore the Spanish Cross, resolutely kept everyone out, except for two conductresses who gave us strawberries and generally mothered us.   We had three Red Cross parcels with us, which our guard assured us would be taken away when we reached Dulag. They would, he said, be quite unnecessary there because: "*In Oberursel ist alles gut.   Essen gut, trinken gut, schlaffen gut.*—At Oberursel everything is fine.   You eat, drink and sleep well." But we rather doubted it and decided to eat as much as we could before we arrived.   It was a lovely summer day and all along the Rhine from the still smoking ruins of Cologne to Bingen, where we changed for Frankfurt, we ate tinned stews, biscuits, jam and chocolate.   It was just as well in view of what was to come.

When we arrived at Oberursel Aicken's knee had done about enough for the day and the guard, who was a decent enough chap, tried to get a car from the camp, but they refused and so we had to trundle out in a tram. A corporal from the camp met us on the tram and took us one stop past the place so that we would approach it from behind and not be able to speak to any British before we had been interrogated.   He was effusively hail-fellow-well-met, but his motives were transparent, his job being to build up a sense of relaxation and confidence in the goodwill of our kindly hosts in which we would subsequently give, without hesitation, any information which might be requested.   He told us that now we were in the hands of the Luftwaffe we would be all right, and outlined the alleged pleasures of Dulag Luft—the football and cricket, the walks in the country, the Red Cross food. He commiserated with us on our injuries and tried to sow a few seeds of discontent by wondering why RAF and Army prisoners always seemed to quarrel.   His act was not a success and we finally arrived in the camp weary, but strongly uncollaborative.

We were separated at once and I was searched by the unsavoury corporal.   I had hidden my illicit possessions in my Red Cross parcels, which were taken away and put into the communal store, although I did manage to retrieve some of the escape kit later.   Aicken had stuck all his stuff in his crotch with sticking plaster and he got away with the lot. so security must have been slack. I was then shut up, and there is no doubt that the first time someone turns the key in the lock and clearly does not mean to unlock it, except at his convenience, you are in no doubt as to your status; as a prisoner you feel lonely and helpless. However, the room—you could scarcely call it a cell—was clean and bright and had a table and chair, and sheets on the bed, although the window was barred and shuttered to prevent any contact with other Kriegies. So, there being nothing else to do, I sat back to await the interrogation which was sure to follow.

The interrogators at Dulag used normal, though happily not violent, techniques. Their methods were well known to the RAF and aircrew were warned about them. The rule was that you must give only your name, rank and number, which by the Geneva Convention is all that a prisoner can be required to give. This rule is simple and if followed it is infallible, but in the hands of an experienced interrogator it is all too easy to be led into conversation. Then one harmless question leads to another and then another and then to one which matters and which is phrased in such a way that if you refuse to reply, the answer can be inferred from the refusal.

Nothing happened until the next morning when an officer walked in. He was courteous and wished me "Good Morning". It was, he said, a fine day. We chatted a little about the weather, and so of course I had already broken rule number one and was standing into danger. Eventually he came to the point by saying that he just wanted a few details so that he could inform the International Red Cross that I was safe. Thereupon he produced the notorious false Red Cross form on which you were asked to fill in details such as your squadron number, base, type of aircraft and commanding officer's name, but we had been warned about this—not that it needed much seeing through—and so I filled in my name and number and put a line through the rest, at which he looked pained:

"I must have these details so that the Air Ministry can be informed of your safety."

"The Air Ministry requires only my name and number."

"But I assure you, all these details are absolutely necessary. There is no question of giving military information. Look, the Red Cross...Think how your family must be worrying."

This cut no ice, as I had already written home from

Düsseldorf. "I am sorry, I can only give the information which I have written down."

"But you don't understand. I have spoken with hundreds of RAF officers—Wing Commanders, even Group Captains—and they have all given these details. Look."

He produced a long and doubtless false list, impressively headed by Wing Commander R R Tuck, DSO, DFC, showing squadron numbers and so on. I shrugged my shoulders and he began to affect exasperation:

"Look, I will show you messages from the Air Ministry."—and out came a sheaf of typed telegrams, purporting to have originated in London, one of which read: "Request information concerning Sgt — of No. — Spitfire squadron, last seen in action over the Channel 10/4/42."

I thought it was time to try a small insult: "Anyone can use a typewriter."

"You—you would accuse me of forgery? Me, a German Officer! I don't believe you know how a British Officer should behave at all. I assure you I have spoken with high officers of the Royal Air Force. None of them—"

"Perhaps I know how a British Officer should behave better than you do. I've been one for two years."

At that he gave up and retired muttering. Evidently the first round was over, but it had got us nowhere. Not long after, however, another officer appeared who was older, more senior—a captain, tall and rather smooth. He had a patronising manner and treated me like a schoolboy. After the usual platitudes he came to the point:

"Now let me see, Mr Morison—it is Mr Morison, isn't it? When were you shot down?"

"I don't know." This was strictly true as I had lost count of dates.

"Oh, come now, you must know that—No? Well perhaps I can jog your memory a little. On 30 May there was a big raid on Cologne. Were you on that? Two nights later there was a raid on Essen. On 25 June a thousand of your bombers raided Bremen—did you know that?"

"Did they? How interesting."

He must surely have known when I came down, so presumably these questions were just for softening up, or for seeing whether I would lie, but it strengthened my morale to learn that we had put a thousand aircraft on Bremen.

"How were you shot down? Was it flak or a fighter?"

"I am sorry. I can't answer any questions of a military nature."

He tried from various angles, then said, angrily:

"Well, I will tell you something. You were flying a Wellington, and you had a collision."

"Did I?"

Smoothly: "Now, what were the names of your crew?"

"I have already told you I can't answer questions like that."

"But you don't understand, there can be no question of this being military information ."

"Then why are you so anxious to know?"

Angrily: "Now listen. You are being very trying. You must understand that you are a prisoner of war now. That makes a difference you know. We will give you another chance later."

Then, standing in the doorway and trying to look sinister: "We have plenty of time, you know."

"So have I."—which was painfully true.

He stormed out, shouting for the *Posten* (Guard), and ordered him to put me in the new jail, where I soon found myself in much less comfortable quarters, no doubt intended to impress on me the folly of my ways. I was now in a very definite cell, one of about fifty in a new building prepared for the ever increasing flood of prisoners which marked the rising effort of the RAF. It was some ten feet by five. There was a bed with two blankets (but no sheets this time), a stool and a table.

I was given a week in which to cool off and it was a week of desperate hunger and feeling of being abandoned (that was the idea, of course). Hunger is at its worst, so far as the sensation is concerned, when it is imposed suddenly. In a few days I had gone from the fat of the land in England via a reasonable sufficiency in Düsseldorf to this Dulag daily diet of four thin slices of bread with a very little margarine and jam, seven or eight potatoes and a plate of watery soup. It was not starvation, but it was very unpleasant. My watch had been taken away, and it became physically painful wondering when the next food would arrive, listening for the rattle of buckets and waiting while the procession worked its way along the passage, stopping at each cell. At first, when at last it arrived, I would peel the dirty old potatoes and cut out the bad bits, but such refined eating habits couldn't long survive the pangs of hunger. Soon I was going back over the rejects, eating the less bad parts and then finally eating the lot. Later in the war I peeled turnip peelings thrown out by the cookhouse to get a little more to eat, but Dulag was my introduction to feeling seriously hungry.

It was hard to occupy the time. I couldn't see out of the window and I was not allowed to read, or shave, or see other prisoners on the way to the lavatory. I spent hours trying to foresee what would happen at the next interview. I tried physical jerks and exercising my arm, but it would scarcely move and was excruciating when it did. I tried lying on the bed and visualising something pleasant like flying a glider, but none of these ploys distracted attention for long from the main question, which was when would the next meal arrive. Soon I was wondering whether it would not be better to give the names of my crew, which seemed to be the only information they really wanted. I still did not know what had happened to them but hoped they might be free. In that case knowledge of their names would help the Germans, but we had been down for a month and I am ashamed to say that I debated how long it was worth starving to maintain a principle. Had I then known what real maltreatment of prisoners is like I might have realised how well off I was and not been such a softy, but all I knew then was that I was miserable.

At long last the tall, patronising captain strode in, over-flowing with good humour:

"Good morning, Mr Morison. How are you? How is your shoulder? I am sorry you were injured. *Posten!* Open the window! I am sure you would like some fresh air, Mr Morison. Look out. Yes, look. There are your friends playing cricket. Now, I am sure you would like to shave and perhaps read a book. *Posten!* See that this officer has a book.

"Now, about the names of your crew. Perhaps you can give them to me...What? But I have already told you that this is not military information. Now listen, you have been very difficult. You must remember that you are very young and you are a prisoner. I didn't at all like your manner the last time we met. You must be careful what you say and how you say it. *C'est le ton qui fait la musique, n'est ce pas?* You understand French?"

I thought it best to deny any knowledge of French, and with that he departed, leaving me with an open window, a book and the right to shave. In this comparative comfort I passed the next few days until suddenly one morning a corporal came in and told me to get ready to go into the camp. Apparently the match was over, and as far as I could see there was no score. Outside in the passage I met my opponent and as we passed I said: "They're taking me away," which he must have taken as a cry for help, as he hastened to assure me that I was only going into the camp.

After the cells the camp was luxury. There was a room labelled 'Officers' Mess' and there were hot showers, conventional beds and plenty of Red Cross food. When about a hundred and fifty prisoners had accumulated they were moved on, but the Germans kept a small, long term staff of British officers to look after the new arrivals and so there was even an office with a notice over the door saying 'Adjutant'. It felt quite like home. Maybe I was only trying to dispel alarm and despondency, but I wrote to my father in glowing terms: "Here it is much more comfortable and the food would be good even in England. Tell Mize not to worry, there is no drink or women here." Evidently I was being pretty free with my father's money, as I asked him to give wedding presents to the value of £15 to two of my friends (about £300 each in 1990s money). "Pay you some day," I said cheerfully. I also asked him to send a pound to the person who had packed my parachute. He wrote to the station commander at Elsham, who replied that it was forbidden to make gifts to service personnel, but he could make a donation to the RAF Benevolent Fund, which was pretty stuffy, seeing that it was the custom to give something to the person who packed your parachute. Needless to say I didn't mention the interrogation, and anyway it would have been censored.

The greatest comfort of being in the camp was to have human company, so that it was no longer just me against the Third Reich (or what Kriegies, to the intense annoyance of the Germans, referred to as the 'Third and Last Reich'). Dulag was a unique community in that everyone had the common characteristic of having been shot down within the past few weeks and now was their first opportunity to tell someone about it. But there are a limited number of ways in which you can get shot down, so after a while conversation tended to pall. Some of the talk was of adventures before capture and included accounts of help given in enemy occupied countries, but of course we only heard about the cases which failed, or worse still were betrayed, and so perhaps we got an unfair view of the immensely brave people who operated the escape lines.

After I had been in the camp about a fortnight the first of my interrogators—the one with the false Red Cross form—poked his head into the room and called:

"Flight Lieutenant Morison?   Ah, Mr Morison, you are from 103 Squadron, are you not?"

"No," I lied hastily, "perhaps it's Sergeant Morison you want."

Fortunately he went away, and I had time to collect my wits. But soon he was back, and, ignoring the embarrassing point about 103 Squadron, he reopened the question of the names of my crew. He assured me that they were all dead and that he only wanted to inform the Air Ministry of their names. I couldn't see why they were so desperately anxious to know these names, but anyway I said that the Air Ministry would have to wait, whereupon I was accused of being a heartless beast.

After two more days of bickering he produced a list of dead which included all my crew and so, as there seemed to be no further purpose in remaining silent, I gave him the names to get rid of him, but no doubt I was wrong to have done so. Give nothing but your name, rank and number. There to this day are the names in my log book: Sgt Traquaire, Sgt Walters, Sgt Grieve, F/Sgt Coxon. Sadly I scarcely knew them, had flown with them only three times in the ten days I was at Elsham, and now they were dead.

The news brought back memories of those barking dogs and pistol shots. Had one of them been shot resisting arrest? I would never know.

The camp had been nearly empty when I arrived, but after a month it had filled up and we were "purged" to Stalag Luft III, the main Luftwaffe camp at Sagan in Silesia.

The three hundred mile train journey lasted twenty four hours and took us deeper and deeper into enemy territory. As the miles rolled by the chance of escape seemed ever more remote, while the prospect of the barbed wire closing irrevocably behind me grew nearer. It was a pretty miserable journey, although at least we went in coaches, not cattle trucks. Some people passed the time playing cards, while others took what would probably be their last look at the wide world for unknown years to come.

There were eight of us in the compartment, but at least I managed to scramble up onto the luggage rack and stretch out to sleep.

CHAPTER FIVE

Stalag Luft III

The Camp

SO on 28 July, 1942, we arrived at Stalag Luft III.

It lay on the outskirts of Sagan, a small country town some one hundred miles south east of Berlin, and as we shambled up from the railway station what might well be our home for the rest of the war presented a drab prospect. The officers' compound consisted of nine wooden huts on a one hundred by two hundred yards patch of dirty barren sand. It was surrounded by a double row of barbed wire with a wooden 'trip rail' ten yards inside it. At intervals along the wire were Goon Boxes on stilts and we knew that if you crossed the rail the Goons in the Boxes would shoot. On one side was a slightly larger sergeants' compound and on another was the *Kommandantur* (the German quarters), while the horizon in every direction was restricted by dark gaunt pine trees.

The huts each had ten rooms, holding ten people, plus two tiny single rooms for senior officers. There was a lavatory with just sufficient capacity to last while we were locked in for the night and a kitchen with a small coal stove, but no running water. One of the huts was the camp kitchen, from which the Goon rations were issued, and there were two wash houses where six hundred of us queued for four taps and twenty lavatory seats. Needless to say the queue for the loos was seldom long because the smell was too evil to allow any but the hardiest to linger.

This apparently drab and featureless place held some surprises for new arrivals. In the first hut I entered I was greeted by the sight of a large, dark man emerging from a hole in the floor, stark naked, covered in sand and brandishing what appeared to be a spear. It would became quite normal, once you got used to it, to see a group sitting in the open on a sunny afternoon singing to an accordion and notice the two in the middle discreetly uncover a hole in the ground and disappear into it; or you might pass a couple of sunbathers sitting on a tree stump with half of their conversation coming from the ground beneath.

I quickly learnt that these phenomena related to the main

71

industry at Sagan, which was escaping.

Every Kriegie was born equal. He arrived with the clothes he wore and that was all, but soon began to acquire possessions; some crockery and books, a chair maybe, or a picture. He also formed relationships, so that society divided into cliques: those who played bridge, or music, or football; those who escaped, or brewed alcohol, or ran the theatre. Thus it was not easy for the new Kriegie to integrate. You can be generous if you have nothing, or if you have more than enough, but if you have painfully acquired just a very little, sharing it with a newcomer is not so welcome. If you had a room where harmony reigned it was a priceless blessing for you had to eat, sleep, cook and wash with these same nine people seven days a week. The furthest you could get apart was two hundred yards. If you thought someone was a right bastard, or even if his breath smelt, you couldn't tell him to his face, and only with difficulty could you move to another room. Diplomacy was at a premium, but its counterpoint was a nicely developed art of innuendo and polite insult.

All had arrived equal, but they soon diverged. Some decorated their rooms, built themselves furniture, kept the place clean and occupied themselves physically and intellectually, while others—not many, fortunately—lived more or less in squalor and spent their time leaning against a stove for which someone else had found the fuel: it was not unlike the world outside.

During the month I arrived at Sagan 30,000 Jews were rounded up in Paris and gassed in Auschwitz; 7708 Russian prisoners of war were buried in a mass grave at Kovno; Hitler visited Auschwitz and asked to see beatings. That was another world of which we were mercifully unaware. The thirty three letters which I wrote home from Sagan over the next year convey the flavour of the very different life we led under the protection of the Lutwaffe. They may seem over-cheerful sometimes, but that was to avoid alarm and despondency at home, and I may appear a bit of an old woman from the quantity of domestic detail, but the business of housekeeping and generally keeping body and soul together was of major importance and absorbed a large part of our time.

Here are some extracts:

I wrote to Grandpére [in Lausanne] *and asked him to send me a toothbrush.*

. . .

I wrote to the bank a few weeks ago and asked them to buy Savings Certificates.

. . .

We have a fuschia in a flower pot, which we bought, and a heather plant in a Wurst tin. The latter I call my grouse moor and I shall probably go shooting on it tommorrow.

. . .

No I have not had any stomach trouble. You must have misconstrued something I said.

. . .

I have since put the contents [of a clothing parcel] to good use. It is very pleasant to have a few nice things again. The vests are the bees' knees, the distinction of a similar pattern being shared only by W/Cmdr Tuck.

. . .

The things to put in every parcel are toothbrushes, shaving soap, socks, razor blades. Have you sent any hand-kerchiefs or face flannels?

. . .

Please send some dish cloths, dusters and tea towels.

It was not all so dull. For example there were many references to theatre productions in which I was involved:

I am acting in a play which we are producing shortly. You probably remember it, French without Tears. I am the girl with the loose morals. It will be good fun I think.

. . .

Dramatic activities are pretty well developed here, as a matter of fact we get about two or three shows of one sort or another in a month, as well as German films.

. . .

I haven't had much space to talk about French Without Tears so far. We are putting it on on Monday for a week. It

*has been very good fun producing it and I think it will be a
success. There are some good fellows in the cast and it fills
in the time well. As I have said, I am the popsy.*

· · ·

*After sundry hold ups and vicissitudes we have at last pre-
sented* French without Tears. *It has been on for two nights
and we have another three to go. All things considered it is a
very good production. The stage hands have built a fine set,
depressingly fine really. We got the Highland, Greek and
Bavarian costumes from Berlin and a few suits which belong
to people here. The ladies' dresses are improvised with the
native ingenuity of the* Kriegsgefangene *and might be
straight from Bond Street. Among the personalities seen on
the first night* were the Kommandant and German officers,
Charles Cochrane, James Agate and P/O Prune.

· · ·

We are doing French without Tears *in the sergeants'
theatre at present. It is better there, with a decent sized
stage and an audience of two or three hundred. It is going
very well and makes a pleasant break. We have just finished
a show here featuring the band as the principal component.
Scene, a night club, with the band at the back of the stage
and the guests, who included some remarkably interesting
characters, wandering on and off at the front. The atmosphere was most realistic—band in red uniforms and the
blokes in tails, party spirit generally. Altogether it was a
great success.*

· · ·

*I am unable to wear the hat you sent as my hair is very
long for stage purposes and the result is altogether too much
like a WAAF to be decent. We did the last one act play I
mentioned last Tuesday and it was quite successful—I am also
learning to tap dance for the next all star, all dancing, all
singing super show.*

· · ·

*I became involved about half way through the rehearsals in
another play* [as Myra Arundel]. *It is* Hay Fever, *one of Coward's earlier efforts.*

· · ·

I know Vivian Kelly well, he is a force in the local theatre world and is master of the chorus in which I dance at present.

We were fortunate to have other highly talented people in the theatre, several of whom became famous after the war, such as Rupert Davies, as Simenon's *Maigret.*

It may seem amazing that we had the materials to build a convincing stage set, or that we could hire costumes from Berlin, but Article 17 of the Geneva Convention says: "Belligerents shall encourage as much as possible the organisation of sporting and intellectual pursuits by prisoners of war". It was also expedient for the Germans to do so, for they thought—poor things—that a Kriegie busy in the theatre was a Kriegie who was not down a tunnel. Maybe so, but the deafening din coming from the stage might have been arranged specially to drown the sound of illicit activity beneath. We had a form of money (described in Chapter 9), to pay for the costume hire and to cap it all was the Kriegie's genius for improvisation, born of necessity. Anyway, Sagan was not a concentration camp; it was a home for temporary guests of the Luftwaffe.

There was also quite a bit in my letters about food, which show that these were days of plenty when we were on full parcels, ie, one a week:

We are all set for Christmas now with plenty of parcels, some beer (untasted as yet) and a suitable tree. I have been cooking again and have contrived some tasty new dishes, notably a jam tart, which included making the jam.

. . .

Christmas passed off in the customary manner with the consumption of large quantities of food and beer. Our dinner menu, so far as I can remember [this was written on 31 December] *was Hors d'oeuvres, Mixed Grill, Christmas Pudding, Mince Pies, Trifle, Biscuits, Cheese, Confectionery and Dried Fruits.*

Of course, we didn't always eat like that!

On two occasions I sent some coded information. The first was rather light hearted:

I hear Lord Millerstone of Tully Fergus is none too well.

ısin, or some such relation, is here and is none too
about the family welfare.

was written in December 1942, when the Russians were
rious at Stalingrad and the Allies were sweeping
ımel out of Africa, and was intended to convey that the
rmans were discouraged. To interpret it you would have
eded to know that shortly before the war we had staying
ıth us, when on holiday in a place called Tully Fergus in
erthshire, a young German called Carl Steinmüller. He was
ın arrogant and unpleasant young man—the worst possible
example of the 'Hitler Youth'—and we knew him as 'Milord
Steinmüller', which translates into English as 'Millerstone'.

The second attempt was more serious and might well have
got me shot for espionage. The censor could never have
interpreted it, but he might have smelled a rat and caused
some difficult questions to be asked. We had noticed a new
type of Heinkel bomber flying over the camp from the local
airfield. The classic Heinkel was the twin engined III with
which the Luftwaffe started the war and used extensively
against Britain, but the one which we were now seeing had
four engines in two pairs. My brother's job in RAF
Technical Intelligence was to get details of German aircraft
so I wrote him this cryptic message:

There are some interesting old ox carts here [this was
true]. *They are similar to the one we saw in Rae's shed, but I
have lately seen some which have four oxen yoked together in
two pairs* [this was not true].

To interpret this you needed to know that my brother and I
had visited the Royal Aircraft Establishment at Farnborough,
commonly known as the RAE, where we had inspected a
captured Heinkel III. Actually my brother failed to interpret
the message (he never was any good at crosswords), but he
recognised that there was something there and sent the letter
on to the appropriate department, but heard no more. The
aircraft in question was in fact the Heinkel 177, but was never
a success, mainly because of trouble with the linking together
of two twelve-cylinder Daimler Benz engines to make a
twenty-four cylinder unit in each wing. Only a few were built
and fewer still saw operational service. One was shot down
near Hindhead, where my brother was able to inspect it,

which made my little exercise in amateur espionage somewhat redundant.

Letters home commented frequently on the state of my shoulder. The first of these said:

There is an English masseur here who is at work on my arm. He is good and I expect a month will see it near normal again.

If I really believed that then I was grossly over-optimistic because it was almost totally paralysed, but three months later I revealed something nearer the truth after I had been chopping up tree stumps for firewood:

The bicep muscles, which were originally the worst damaged and the most reluctant to start work again, are now in action, albeit weakly. Local opinion gives it that my collar bone was probably fractured in the first place, but the various X-rays having been lost no one quite knows. Compared with the depressing sight which confronted me when the bandages were first removed in hospital it is now a miracle of efficiency as a limb. It is certainly wonderful how it has gradually developed from a bone, scarcely flesh covered and quite incapable of automation.

In late 1942 a new and larger compound was constructed to house the growing flood of prisoners:

I went over to a new compound which is being built for us last Monday to help clear a sports ground. The place is not finished yet, but will be more pleasant when we get there. The trees are left standing, the rooms are smaller and the furniture new. The soil looks richer so perhaps gardening will be more successful.

It was not until five months later, at the end of March 1943, that we moved to the new compound and I wrote detailed descriptions:

In my last letter I described the outline of the room we live in. As you will have realised most of the space, especially on the walls, is occupied by furniture and leaves little room for works of art. However there are a lute and a guitar sus-

the wall when not in use and one or two
he inmates. Virtually everything is made of
o the stuffing of the mattresses, which is wood
a rather uniform colour of yellow or yellow-
des the room, relieved here and there by a
nket or a row of books. There are many schools
n how to keep a room, varying from the drawing
to the junk shop. We favour a mild state of chaos.
within the compass of the room, peel potatoes and
y, paint pictures and make frying pans, play lutes
res. If you try and maintain a polish on the table
a circumstances you have no time left to devote to
lse. As a result the table under the window bears
ment 4 tins of Rothmans cigarettes, 10 packets of
itto, 2 books and a sheet of calculations on higher
rubber, handkerchief adapted as headwear, a
ble knife, 3 ashtrays, some odd books, an unidenti-
board box, a pair of sunglasses and so on. [Line
eted by the censor.] Outside the window is our
garden, then a road as yet half made, then nothing in
ar. Beyond are pine trees which form the principal

ooked forward to receiving books from home:

book parcels have been arriving in a veritable flood of
bout 30 books altogether: North Cape, Aesop and
& Amber. Far more than I can read at once, but they
eep and many other people enjoy them.

ng the books were works on accountancy. Before the
here had been an idea that I would become a Chartered
untant and join an uncle's firm, and now my father
uaded me that I should start to study for the exams,
ough goodness knows why when there were so many
er more exciting things to do. Then my uncle, thinking
ave time after the war, contrived to get me articled. I
te:

There is no limit to the surprises in life is there? There
u are one moment, nothing in particular happening, and
e next moment you are an articled clerk. The immediate
ery round the room was: "How much do you get paid?"

That sounded all right until some bright character said that it was I who did the paying.

I asked for colour to cheer up the drab surroundings and one day with a book parcel came some colour prints:

...many of them now adorn the walls of our room. I like the one by Monet of the lily pool under the bridge in particular. General approval was expressed when they arrived and your reputation for sending the right thing, already high, was considerably enhanced.

We had tobacco parcels. I did not smoke, but cigarettes were the universal currency, and not least for bribing Goons. My father sent quality as well as quantity, mostly Players No. 3. A person in our hut had a roulette wheel and naturally the stakes were in tobacco. Being a Wing Commander he had a room to himself and his walls were stacked high with cigarette packets. If you wanted proof that the odds are loaded in favour of the bank, that was it.

We had music. Not only concerts, but many people had guitars and there was the twelve stringed lute which hung in our room. It belonged to Nick Pollock, but nine of the strings were redundant as he could never manage more than two or three at once. 'Wings' Larkin had a guitar and often played and sang for us. He was an Australian, which may explain why we had never heard some of his songs before. One of my favourites went something like this:

'Her name was Lil, she was a beauty,
She lived in a house of ill reputy,
And men came from far and near to see
Lil-eye-an in her déshabille.

'Lil was comely, she was fair,
She had stacks of yellow hair,
But she drank too deep of the demon rum,
She smoked hashish and op-eye-um.

'Now Lil-eye-an grew thinner and thinner,
Due to lack of prot-eye-n in 'er.
So she consulted her ph-eye-sician
To prescribe for her condition.

'She ate liver, she ate yeast,
But still her clientele decreased.
Now every night before she goes to sleep,
She prays to the Lord her soul to keep,
In a penthouse on Fifth Avenue.'

Then there was another, but this one had a cockney
intonation so can't have come from down under:

'There was a bleedin' sparrer
Lived up a bleedin' spout.
There came a bleedin' rainstorm
Wot washed the bleeder out.
Then as that bleedin' sparrer
Lay sprawlin' on the grass,
'E told that bleedin' rainstorm
To come and kiss 'is arse.
But before that bleedin' sparrer
Could crawl back in his snuggery,
There came a bleedin sparrer 'awk
Wot fucked 'im up to buggery.
Then came a bleedin' sporting type
Wot 'ad a bleedin' gun,
And shot that bleedin' sparrer
Right up 'is bleedin' bum.
Now the moral of this story
Is plain to all and one
It's them's as lives up bleedin' spouts
Don't get no bleedin' fun.'

Simple stuff, but magic as sung to Wings Larkin's guitar.
He also sang that beautiful song which, despite its innocence
by today's standards, you can still find only in the most
complete of the 'Complete' works of Rudyard Kipling[1], and
which starts off:

'I've taken my fun where I've found it;
I've rogued and I've ranged in my time;
I've had my pickin' o' sweethearts,
An' four o' the lot was prime.
One was an 'arf caste widow,

[1]The complete poem is in Appendix B.

One was a woman from Prome,
One was the wife of a *jemadar-sais*,
An' one is a girl from home.'

Wings Larkin, being Australian, inevitably sang 'Waltzing Matilda', as well as 'Frankie and Johnnie', 'Abdul the Bul Bul Amir' and other less printable numbers.

So, we had housekeeping and we had theatre and books and tobacco and study and music and just chatting to one another (sometimes known as 'dog stuffing'); there was no excuse to be bored. Then of course we had games. Bridge for example, but other people playing bridge can drive you mad when you can't get away from them. We did not have cricket—not enough space—but we had football. I don't like football. When the Americans arrived we had baseball. Baseball can drive you mad faster than bridge with its incessant cries of: "Hey, hey, play ball! Pitch 'em up there boy!" and "Strike one, one and one!"—whatever that may mean. But why bother with these things when the greatest game of all was waiting to be played?—the Kriegies' game *par excellence* at which any number could play, any time, any day: Escaping.

The Escaping Scene

A game, did you say? Well, more like a field sport really, for which it had all the right ingredients: action, often in the open air; initiative; competition; excitement; a touch of danger; and, if you got it wrong, real danger. As we were British, naturally the game was played according to the Queensberry Rules, or to be more precise in this case, The Geneva Convention Rules. These rules were simple: Don't use violence. Don't engage in sabotage or espionage. Don't wear German uniform. If you get caught, spend a couple of weeks in the cooler and return to go. These rules held until March 1944 when German patience, stretched by disaster on every front, finally broke. They shot fifty Kriegies who had escaped from Sagan and published a notice addressed "To all Prisoners of War" and ending with the ominous words "Escaping is no longer a sport". Too true. Back in 1942, however, there were no such worries, unless you were unlucky enough to get picked up by the Gestapo—although, even then, if you could get word to the Luftwaffe they would probably be able to rescue you. They hated the Gestapo.

Escaping was an official activity. Indeed, soon after our arrival we were addressed by Group Captain Massey, the Senior British Officer, who made it clear that escaping, and every other form of anti-German activity, had his support— except for insulting them, which, apart from being unbecoming for an officer, was common sense, because you could waste a lot of good escaping time being kept on parade if people booed, hissed and made a nuisance.

Most people tried to escape because they wanted to get home, although there were other motives. Everyone realised the slimness of his chances, because of those seriously prepared to do all the hard work not a tenth would ever see the outside of the wire; and of those who did, maybe two or three out of a hundred got home. All the same it was an objective and perhaps the only really worthwhile one we had. You might occupy your time studying for your future career, or brewing alcohol for your immediate pleasure, but there was a war on in which you had sworn "to be faithful and bear true allegiance to His Majesty King George the Sixth, his Heirs and Successors", and that you would, "as in duty bound, honestly and faithfully defend His Majesty, His Heirs and Successors, in Person, Crown and Dignity against all Enemies." (Phew!)—and to try and get home seemed to be the only way of honouring that oath. The immediate cost to the enemy might not be great, but every man hour of German labour diverted to guarding, searching, floodlighting and wiring camps was one hour less with which to to produce bombs which might land on your home, or guns which might shoot down your friends. It was not much of a contribution to the war effort, but the fact that one was still fighting, even if only very slightly, kept up morale.

While we indulged the human desire to get home, with to some extent a sense of duty, we also occupied a great deal of time. Even if you never got outside the wire it was a lot of fun trying to outwit the opposition (it really was a game, you see). If you did get out there was at least the certainty of a break from the monotony of camp life and, however slender, the wonderful chance that you might actually make it home.

Escaping may have been an official activity, but when I arrived at Sagan it was not strictly organised. There was indeed an Escape Committee, but little discipline. Escape attempts proliferated, often conflicting with one another and resulting in discovery. It was a free for all. This persisted until about Christmas 1942 when there arrived in the camp the person who was to dominate the escaping scene until March 1944, when the Germans shot him. This was Squadron Leader Roger Bushell. Roger had started his escaping career early, his first outing being from Dulag, where they scarcely had time to question him before he hid in a goat's shed on the playing field and eventually reached the Swiss frontier, to be recaptured only a few yards from safety. Recently he had escaped again and had reached Prague, where he stayed in a safe house until picked up by the Gestapo. He had had a brush with them before and when finally they decided to return him to the custody of the Luftwaffe they warned him that if they ever met again it would be their last encounter.

Back in Sagan Roger was put in charge of escaping, and soon the whole scene changed. Gone were the days of private enterprise schemes competing higgledy-piggledy and falling over one another in the process. The business was now directed from the top. If you had a scheme it had to be approved, and if it was approved you could get help from communal resources. Roger was passionate in his determination to defeat the enemy and scenes which he had witnessed on the streets of Prague did nothing to lessen his hatred of the Nazis. But emotion didn't cloud his judgement. He was a barrister, cool, logical and ruthless.

With the Gestapo's warning fresh in his mind he knew the risks which he ran. It was important to conceal his activities, for as well as being dangerous his job would have become impossible had the Germans watched his every move. He was never referred to by his name, but always by his *nom de guerre*, 'Big X'. Melodramatic maybe, but necessary. Roger was one of my heroes.

The Kriegies' most popular means of attack was the tunnel, the alternatives being to cut through the wire or to climb over it—both very dangerous—or to walk through the gate which, although the natural way out, was difficult to arrange. On the Germans' side, their principal defence was the 'ferret'. Ferrets were the brightest of the guards and their business was to roam the camp keeping an eye open for suspicious signs. Clad in blue overalls and usually carrying a three metre steel rod for probing the ground, they were easily recognised, but their movements had to be monitored all the time as they were quite capable of disappearing beneath a hut and then surfacing at some inconvenient moment. Wherever any clandestine activity was in progress we would have a Kriegie on watch, and if a ferret approached he would utter the warning cry "Goons up". (The ferrets sometimes shouted it themselves, which belies General Wavell's story in 'TEE EMM' about the Germans lacking a sense of humour. They have one alright, it's just a bit different from ours.) As the warning cry died away you might see the pages of a magazine quietly turned over to hide a half forged document, or perhaps a saw thrown under a pillow and the sawdust swept into the stove. Someone walking casually past the intruding Goon might have a wad of *Reichsmarks* in his pocket, but all would probably be well because anything out of sight was usually safe, except when there was an organised search party.

Nevertheless, there could be awkward moments: one day when I was in my room sewing trousers for an escape, *Feldwebel* Glemnitz, the NCO in charge of camp security, who had somehow escaped notice, put his head in the window. Panic—but then: "That's all right *Herr* Morison, I was just looking round. It would never do if you were up to something that is not allowed, but I know you wouldn't do anything like that." He probably thought of me as 'Diana', a rather effeminate looking young man with long hair and a taste for playing the female lead in the theatre, but at least he had the courtesy to call me *Herr* Morison. When my heart had slowed down a little I felt rather pleased, for Glemnitz wasn't stupid. *Hauptmann* Pieber, who was one of the camp officers, certainly thought of me as 'Diana' and frequently addressed me as such.

Not only had the ferrets to be watched, but a constant check had to be kept on all the Goons who were in the camp. To this end a twenty four hour watch was kept on the gate and a record made of all comings and goings. The watchman, who by RAF analogy was known as the Duty Pilot, was tolerated by the Germans, although they could not have suppressed him had they tried. Maybe they did not want to, because on at least one occasion he was useful to them: One day Glemnitz was looking through the Duty Pilot's log, to the accompaniment of some friendly banter, when he noticed that a ferret had been booked out in the small hours of the morning, long before his spell of duty should have finished. The hapless ferret spent some days under arrest and when finally he returned to the camp, a very angry man, he upbraided the Duty Pilot. "I'm sorry about that," was the reply. "The next time you want to leave early let me know and I'll book you out at your proper time."

Because the soil was almost pure sand tunnels were easy to dig, but the sand was loose and so they had to be shored up. Fortunately, the necessary materials were ready to hand in the shape of bed boards, the transverse slats in the wooden bunks on which our mattresses rested. You could take out one board and not notice it. You could take two or three and it still wasn't too bad, but after that the the sagging mattress began to look like a sea serpent and the bed became progressively less habitable. In the days of freelance tunnelling you might have been able to protect your own bed, but after Big X had taken a grip he would send round the Little Xs, his representatives in each hut, to commandeer bed boards on the basis of one or two per bed and, a bit later, one or two more.

The sand was easy to excavate so long as you had enough bed boards to shore it up, but then it had to be disposed of. The easiest was to scatter it under a hut, especially as that was where tunnels usually started, but then it was obvious that a tunnel was somewhere near and a ferret, probing the soft sand with his steel rod, was likely to find it. This problem proved intractable until we moved to the new compound, when a brilliant solution was found. One idea which had been tried in the old compound was the mole tunnel in which two Kriegies were sealed in and one dug the sand away in front while the other piled it into the tunnel behind him. There were two catches, however. First, you couldn't keep this up for long, so the tunnel had to start near the wire, but worse still, the sand stored at the back inevitably took more space than the hole from which it had come so that the working space shrank inexorably. Moling was not a success.

One determined Kriegie had the idea of starting a tunnel from the pit beneath the latrines. It was a brilliant idea, if unsavoury in execution. The latrines were fairly near to the wire and so the tunnel would be short and the sand could simply be spread around the pit to mix with the excrement,

which later would be pumped out into the ox-drawn tank
wagons which emptied these hell holes. Best of all, who in
their wildest moments would imagine that anyone would be
crazy enough to go tunnelling in a pit beneath a dozen holes
from which descended a stream of—well, a stream. The urge
to escape suppressed many civilised inhibitions, but sadly
this brave idea failed.

If you did not tunnel you could try the wire, and of course
that would be a lot less trouble than digging for weeks and
weeks and then being discovered. But whether you fancied
cutting through it, or climbing over it, you were asking to be
shot unless you had some very bright idea. Kriegies were
nothing if not creative thinkers, and two such ideas did
emerge, both of which got their creators outside the wire,
although, alas! not all the way home. The first scheme was
the result of brilliant reasoning by a couple of Kriegies who
calculated that, as seen from a Goon Box, the line of posts
forming the fence would merge into a solid mass, blocking
the view of anything immediately next to the wire. Thus, if
you could get to the wire without being seen and then lie
close to it you would be invisible and could cut your way
through at leisure. The theory was impeccable, but would
anyone be brave enough to put it into practice? Ken Toft and
Bill Nichols were, and they did, and it worked. First they had
to get from the trip rail to the shelter of the fence, and for
that the classic tactic was a diversion to distract the sentry's
attention while something happened which he must not see.
It might be two people having an argument leading to a fight,
or someone appearing to act suspiciously, but as sentry work
is tedious anything interesting soon attracted attention. So it
was that in a couple of seconds, while the Goon looked away,
Ken and Bill darted across from the trip rail, lay down by the
wire and quietly cut their way through. I do not know where
the wire cutters come from. You did not ask questions which
which were not your business, but maybe there was a pair of
skates which would never see the ice again. Skates made very
good tool steel.

This wire job was from the old compound, so when the new
compound was built the Goon boxes were designed with a
platform overhanging the wire from which the sentry could
see along it. As usual the defence had caught up with the
attack, but to Johnny Stower's quick eye here was an
opportunity to get even. He realised that if once he could get

A De Havilland DH 82 Tiger Moth.

A Hawker Hart in the RAF Museum, Hendon.

A Westland Lysander. *(IWM CH1194.)*

Safely back. A Wellington of 103 Squadron comes home with the dawn.

The cockpit of a Wellington, showing the bomb master switch (A), and the closely placed landing light switch (B) and bomb door control (C) which caused the author so much trouble over Dieppe. In this illustration the landing light switch is shown with a safety catch, which must have been a later modification. *(HMSO.)*

Room 5 Block 68   Stammlager Luft 3.   July 12th 1942.

Above: A typical room in Stalag Luft III.
Below: After the show—the 'girls' in *French Without Tears*.
Author, second from left; Vivian Kelly, centre.

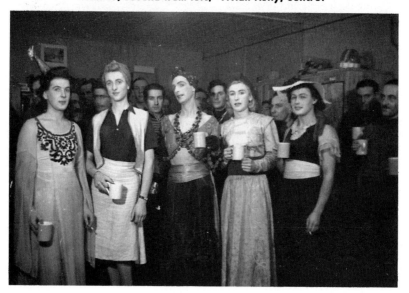

Lorne Welch.
Portrait by F/Lt Alex Cassie, Sagan, 1942.

Above: The air pump designed by Lorne Welch for tunnel 'Harry' is inspected by a ferret after the 'Great Escape' in March 1944. *(IWM HU21218.)*
Below: A selection of forged passes. *(IWM HU21214.)*

under this overhanging platform the sentry would be unable to see him and he could climb over the wire with impunity. A diversion would distract the sentry while he popped under the protective cover and it would be done at dusk, just before the flood lights were switched on, so that even if the Goon in the next box saw him the chance of his shooting straight would be slight. Again the theory seemed impeccable. Johnny was an inveterate escaper and not one to be put off by a bit of danger. The scheme worked perfectly and he was up and over in a matter of seconds. No weeks of sweating away in a tunnel for him; all he had used was his brain and his courage. But alas! as he ran for the cover of the trees he tripped and fell. With two machine guns levelled at him it was the end of a brilliant attempt.

Then there were gate jobs, and for those you might try and get out hidden in a cart or a lorry which had come into the compound, but they were always searched as they left and it was an unreliable method. Success was more likely to come from schemes based on meticulous planning, careful observation of the comings and goings of Goons, the production of forged passes and German uniforms, and the services of fluent German speakers. Such schemes, although not guaranteed, might be made to work.

But How to Escape?

Our urge to escape grew stronger by the day. England still seemed very near because there was a constant flow of new arrivals who had been there only a few days previously and who produced conversations like: 'You know "The Snakepit" in Lincoln?' 'Yes.' 'Well, I was there a couple of weeks or so ago having a beer with old George, yes George Finlay. Got the chop the next night, as it happens. Well, George said—.' It was easy to feel that a twist of fortune could take you back home just as easily as it had taken you away. There was not much good war news during most of 1942, but our spirits were volatile and even a small Allied advance would send them soaring. Then the optimists would be saying "Home by Christmas", but sober thought told you that if that was your ambition then you had to escape. But how? Daydreams were unrationed and there was plenty of time for them. Mine centred round liberating a Luftwaffe aircraft and flying home, a dream which had started right back in hospital in Düsseldorf. Of course, in the dream I always landed back at Elsham, a bit overdue maybe, but the CO could scarcely complain and I could see the surprise on everyone's face; I knew the stories I would tell in the mess and I could taste the floods of free beer which would come my way...

Then I found another Kriegie with the same idea. He was Lorne Welch, and when he arrived at Sagan four weeks after me a happy stroke of fate landed us in the same room. Lorne had been shot down while still at OTU and this is his tale:

I joined the RAFVR as a sergeant pilot in 1938, at Woodley, and by the time war started had flown about 150 hours on Miles Magisters and Hawker Harts. After being called up I was given a flying instructor's course on the same aircraft and in December 1939 was posted as an instructor to Elmdon, flying Tiger Moths. This school was civilian run, with both civilian and RAF instructors, but Naval pupils. They were all midshipmen or acting leading naval airmen and were the best group I ever had to teach to fly. Unfortunately this happy time did not last long. as after four months I was posted to Brough, on the Humber. It was Tiger Moths again and also Blackburn B2s. These were less good aircraft but had the merit that instructor and pupil sat side by side, which made teaching easier.

After a year at Brough my commission came through, but I was kept on at the same job. Finally in, September 1941, I managed to get off instructing and was posted to Cranwell to learn to fly twins, including night flying and astro nav. This seemed to take ages.

In April 1942 I eventually reached an OTU at Finningley, flying Ansons and Wellingtons. My first operation was the 1000 bomber raid on Cologne as co-pilot, followed two days later by a raid on Essen. Finally I got a crew of my own with an English navigator, John Hamilton, and a Canadian rear gunner, wireless operator and bombardier. Our first operation was to Bremen; it was uneventful, which was just as well since it was the first time I had been captain on a night flight of any distance. More training followed with this crew until on 31 July, 1942, we went on our next and last trip, to Düsseldorf. All went smoothly until we were approaching the flak and searchlights over the target, when suddenly tracer started flying past from a night fighter on our tail. There was not much damage at first, but after hectic evasive action, in which we lost height from 14,000 down to 8000 feet, the fighter picked us up again killing Penney, our rear gunner. One engine was now out of action and the hydraulics had failed so that the wheels hung down. We had no airspeed indicator and no intercom. After further evasive action, in which we lost a lot more height, and now heading for home, the fighter finally left us in peace; instead, we had flak from Eindhoven. Our situation was now pretty hopeless, as the Wimpy on one engine and with wheels down simply went on losing height. I jettisoned the bombs, but we continued to sink rapidly. I gave the order to bale out—difficult without the intercom—but by the time anyone was ready we were too low and the only thing left was to try to crash land safely.

We were over Holland, the ground was flat, and there was moonlight, so I was able to pick a suitable place. But when making the final turn to line up with the longest clear space I had that shuddering feeling of being too slow. Stuffing the nose down, I just had time to straighten up before the ground arrived. The aircraft was in one piece, although on its belly, when the dangling wheels collapsed as we touched.

We might have got away and found refuge with the Dutch, but Valensky, my bombardier, had been standing next to me in the cockpit, and as we slid to a noisy halt he fell through the hatch in the floor. The rest of us scrambled out to find him trapped under the fuselage badly injured, but alive. To add to the confusion, flames started to flicker from one engine cowling, but I was able to dowse them with the extinguisher. I gave Valensky morphia from the first aid kit and we tried to free him, but three men cannot lift a Wellington. There was a farmhouse near by, so after sending the navigator and wireless operator off to try to escape I went for help, speaking my bad German. Several people brought long poles as levers but we still could not lift the aircraft. By now I was getting desperate until suddenly a young Dutch girl appeared out of the darkness and with her came her brain. This she used instead of the brawn which we had been expending so ineffectively. She took a look at Valensky and said in excellent English: "Why don't you just dig him out?" Immediately our helpers ran off to fetch spades and in no time we had him free.

Dutch police arrived, soon followed by Germans. They promised me that they would send Valensky to hospital, but insisted that I must go with them as I was under arrest. At this I showed all the anger I could muster, and said that as the captain of the aircraft I was responsible for the safety of my crew and must stay with my bombardier until he was in hospital. To my surprise, they agreed, and we drove off in an ambulance to Tilburg. There I had to leave him, but I could see that he was in the care of kindly nuns, and happily they nursed him back to health.

The Germans took me to the Luftwaffe base at Eindhoven and then by train to Amsterdam. In Holland there was a good chance of finding shelter among friends, so all the time I was looking for ways to escape from my escort, but no opportunity turned up before the train reached Amsterdam. This was the terminus. and while we were still on the platform I saw the empty train start to back out of the station. It was now or never, so I ran to jump through an open door in the last coach, hoping that the train would accelerate out of the station before my guards could stop it. But at the last moment a man appeared in the doorway. I knew my luck was running out fast, so in desperation I made a dash across the tracks and for the first time heard the ominous cry: *"Halt oder wird erschossen!*—Stop or we fire!" I ran on across the lines on to another platform, where I found stairs leading down, I hoped, to an exit. Instead it was a gloomy storeroom with plywood blackout panels over the windows. Pulling one off, I smashed it through the dirty glass, to reveal the main station square of Amsterdam in brilliant sunshine and crowded with people. I kept running, hoping to merge into the crowd. The chasing Germans now started shooting and a girl nearby was hit in the leg, though happily not seriously, so I decided that I had better stop before any innocent Dutch people were killed.

The next few days were spent in a wretched Amsterdam prison until, handcuffed to another English bolter I was taken to the railway station and put on a train to Frankfurt, then a tram to Oberursel and the transit camp Dulag Luft. Three weeks later I arrived at Sagan.

Hanging above my bed I had a small model glider. Lorne asked me about it and that set us talking, soon leading to thoughts about how we might fly home. Lorne had imagination and a lateral thinking mind, so he was the ideal person with whom to explore every detail of this fascinating subject. At first it was all dreams and fantasies and we discussed them endlessly, driving our room mates mad in the process, but slowly we became more practical and finally decided that to fly was not only one of the best ways out of Germany, but for us it was the only way. So far so good. But there was a catch, for first of all it was necessary to get outside the wire and the supply of escape opportunities fell far short of the demand. Bushell had clamped down on tunnels, except for one or two which had a serious chance of success, and so you needed a brilliant idea like Toft and Nichols' or Johnny Stower's, but even Lorne's normally fertile brain was barren. Then came an inspiration: there was a verse from a show in the theatre which went:

> 'Oh, I have got a scheme in mind
> For Tuck and Norman Ryder
> To get to England, flying blind,
> Borne in a cardboard glider.'

Did you say a glider? Yes, a glider. Think. Think. Keep thinking. Could we? Yes, we might. Don't be silly, you can't fly out of the camp in a glider. How would you build it? Where would you hide it? How would you launch it? We kept thinking. Lorne could design it and I knew how to operate it—just to get over the wire of course, but that was all we needed. So we went to see Bushell. He listened attentively, and then said we should work out more detail and if it still seemed practicable he would back us. That was crucial. Without his approval we could not do anything; with it we would have access to all the resources of the escape organisation. It may sound like a hair brained scheme, but later in the war a glider was successfully built in another camp. However, at Sagan it was not to be for something happened which put the idea to the bottom of our priorities.

In March 1943 we made the long awaited move to the new compound like immigrants to a new country, carrying all our possessions on our backs, or in a suitably old-world looking hand cart. We arrived in a wonderland where the ground was scarcely trodden and trees grew among the huts. There were wash basins with shiny taps, lavatories that flushed and bright new furniture, crockery and cutlery. Perhaps the Goons thought that by giving us luxurious accommodation we would opt for the easy life and retire from escaping, but if so they were wrong.

The rooms in the huts were smaller than in the old compound, but I had collected five other people who I hoped would live together in harmony and we set to work to produce order out of chaos. Like an excited schoolboy I could not stop laughing, chattering and pushing furniture about to try to find the ideal layout for the minute space, while at intervals I would rush off to explore the camp and look in on other people to see how they were arranging their rooms.

The compound itself was only about three hundred yards square, but it seemed enormous, and on the first day it was almost possible to feel lost in it. The place was also full of booty, because the builders had left odds and ends of timber, wire, nails and tools lying about, all of which were valuable prizes to be collected and stored away for the future. We were squirrels and hoarded any little object we found in case it might come in useful.

When we moved in, work on the new compound had not been completed so the Germans had to bring in civilian workmen and Russian prisoners of war to finish it. The civilians soon found themselves losing their tools and any bits of clothing which might come in handy for an escape, while to the Russkies we passed whatever food and tobacco we could. Some were Russian airmen who were prisoners of the Luftwaffe and tolerably well treated, although the officers had to work. Most, however, were army prisoners and they were half-starved. It was a nasty shock for us well fed young men when, for the first time in our lives, we saw other men fight for the bits of bread which we were able to throw to them when their guard's attention was diverted.

The Luftwaffe's Russian prisoners were full of life and fun. We weren't supposed to have any contact with them, but we threw them cigarettes and even managed some elementary conversation:

RAF: "Stalin prima."

Russkies (much beaming and smiles): "Churchill prima!"

RAF: "Viva Stalingrad!"

Russkies: "Stalingrad prima!" (Just then the Germans were being driven out of Stalingrad).

The Russkies were quick to respond and would slip us a pickaxe or try to smuggle one of us out of the camp with their party. They were brave, too, for they had far more to lose than us if they were caught. They were working on the roadway outside my window and sometimes it was better than a pantomime. One day I watched while they did nothing despite the exhortations of their guard. Then along came a ferret and tried his hand at getting some work out of them, but they just looked helpless and shrugged their shoulders, as if to say that such a complex job was beyond their simple minds. Then the ferret, exasperated, but convinced of the superiority of the Aryan race, demonstrated the approved Reich method of filling a wheel barrow with sand. In a few moments he had the barrow full, but behind his back broad grins had spread across the Russian faces. Then the ferret stood back as if to say: 'There, that is how a German would do it.'

"Now, you, take it away," ordered the ferret.

"Me?" asked the expressive face of the Russkie, "but that's far too heavy."

"Far too heavy," echoed the faces of his friends.

He made a desperate attempt to lift the barrow, but failed, then another had a go. Amidst a chorus of encouragement from the onlookers he staggered a few yards, then all the sand spilled back onto the ground. Wherever the ferret looked there were signs of distress and voluble advice on how to retrieve the disaster, but behind his back there were chuckles. Russkies one. Goons nil. Viva Stalingrad.

But the Goons could manage a joke too, and a subversive one at that:

Kriegie to guard watching Russian working party: "Hitler. *Ist er verheiratet?—Is he married?"*

Guard: *"Hitler verheiratet? Nein."* Looking round cautiously: *"Hitler. Maschine kaputt!"*

The move to the new compound released a flood of enthusiasm for escape, and in the first few days several quick chances were seized—of which Johnny Stower's climb under the goon box was one—but Bushell was determined that the potential of this virgin ground must not be squandered by ill designed or unco-ordinated attempts and schemes were strictly disallowed unless approved. In particular, there were to be no private enterprise tunnels; instead, three communal tunnels were planned and they were code named 'Tom', 'Dick' and 'Harry'. We had civil engineers in the camp so the tunnels were properly designed and constructed, deep and long. Harry's shaft went down thirty feet and then the tunnel had to run for 330 feet to get outside the wire. They were deep to avoid detection by microphones buried in the sand, or by ferrets with their long steel spikes, but the most important precaution was to ensure that the Goons never saw any sign that tunnelling was in progress.

The two weak points likely to give a tunnel away to a nosey ferret were the entrance, or trap, and the disposal of the sand. All three tunnels had brilliantly concealed traps, the crucial element being that although they started at floor level a ferret crawling about under a hut would see nothing suspicious. The only way to achieve this was to make the entrance where there was concrete or brick from the floor down into the foundations. Every room had a big, heavy coal-burning stove standing on a concrete base and in Hut 104 the stove in one room was first fitted with a flexible chimney pipe and then lifted off its base, still burning. Next the base was cut away and a new one made, which was hinged so that it could easily be lifted to reveal the brick pier beneath,

through which the shaft was cut. When all was complete
there was nothing to show anything different from the stoves
in other rooms. The trap could now be opened and the
workers got in or out in a matter of moments before the stove
was back in place and all was again concealed. That the
stove could be kept burning was vital as otherwise the
occupants of the room would have frozen in winter and such
odd behaviour would soon have given away the secret. These
traps were virtually ferret proof. Tom's was discovered by
misadventure, but Harry's only when the tunnel broke.
Dick's was never discovered and very likely the tunnel is still
there.

On this virgin ground the old practice of dumping sand
under a hut would have been fatal, and so instead a scheme
was devised which involved the use of 'penguins'. A penguin
was a Kriegie who carried inside his trouser legs bags holding
the excavated sand, which he could dribble out by pulling on
a cord. The penguins wandered nonchalantly about the
camp spreading the sand over a wide area, earning their
name from the waddling gait induced by the weight inside
their trousers. The scheme worked, and the Goons, who
knew that a Kriegie started tunnelling almost as soon as his
parachute had opened, became more and more worried every
day that they failed to see so much as a bit of disturbed sand.

Bushell mobilised every skill in the camp towards the
common goal, and by working for the cause you could earn
the chance of escape on a communal scheme like a tunnel.
There were tailors who produced German uniforms and
civilian clothes, draughtsmen who forged passes, engineers
who designed tunnels, contact men who worked on the Goons
to procure illicit goods in exchange for cigarettes or
chocolate; and then there was the Gadget Factory.

Bushell appointed Lorne to run the Gadget Factory, then
Lorne recruited me and a Norwegian pilot, Jens Muller. Our
job was to produce any article which seemed to be no one
else's pigeon, for example a dummy rifle, or—our major
project—the ventilation systems for Tom, Dick and Harry.
Lorne was a brilliant improviser, but he liked to try out his
ideas on what he impolitely described as an ignorant
bystander and that was usually me. Sure enough, if the
ignorant bystander could understand the idea it must be
simple and therefore likely to work, although not all his ideas
worked. One which nearly led to disaster was a rope which

we supplied for hauling sand buckets up from the tunnels. We had experimented with a primitive rope-spinning machine to make rope from string, but it was not much good so we turned to kitbag cords. Unfortunately, they could not just be knotted together, because they had to run over a pulley, and so they had to be spliced. The difficulty was that they were plaited and not many people can splice plaited rope. Lorne worked away until he had devised a splice. We tested it satisfactorily, so we made up the first length and delivered it to the tunnellers, while Lorne rejoiced in the knowledge of another tricky problem solved. Rejoiced, that was, until he was confronted by a furious tunneller who had narrowly escaped death when a splice parted and a bucket of sand plunged thirty feet down the shaft. The reason was that we had only tested the splice in tension, but when it was pushed together, as might happen only rarely, it unravelled. This was not only a narrow escape for the tunneller, but also for the tunnel—for a dead, or seriously injured Kriegie would have been hard to explain away.

The digging teams soon found that their fat lamps were going out for lack of oxygen, and it became obvious that because of the depth and length of the tunnels a powered ventilation system would be needed. This had to be one for the Gadget Factory, but to produce a powered ventilation system for a tunnel which would extend for over a hundred yards needed all Lorne's ingenuity, as well as a formidable inventory of materials including two bed sides, two bed ends, two kit bags, nine coat hooks, four ice hockey sticks, four ping pong bats, soft leather from a flying boot and sundry nails and screws. Bits of beds were fairly easily come by because the camp wasn't yet full, but most materials were scarce. If we used a hockey stick it meant that someone could not play hockey.

As sub-contractors to the tunnelling team it was our job not only to supply the equipment, but to fit it. Getting all the kit safely to the hut where we went to install Harry's pump was quite a problem, and having never seen the entrance before we were amazed when the trap was opened and it was revealed. Thirty feet down the two foot square shaft I at once decided that tunnelling was best left to others, while Lorne was showing signs of claustrophobia, but we did the job and retreated gratefully to the daylight above.

From the bottom of the shaft there had to be pipes to carry

the air along the tunnel, and to make them we employed an uncomplaining American who sat cross legged on the floor for hour after hour cutting the ends off empty food tins with a pair of nail scissors. Straight runs of pipe were bad enough, but to go round corners the ends of the tins had to be cut to precise angles. For this we needed a mathematician and we found him in one of our room mates, 'Food' Braithwaite. 'Food'—pronounced 'Fud'—was so called not because he was greedy (far from it) but because of his Geordie accent, which gave words like 'food' and 'foot' very short *oo*s. He had been hideously burned about the face when his Hampden was shot down by a night fighter, and in his condition he probably had little personal chance of escape, but like so many others he worked for the cause. After the war the RAF kept him on throughout the long and painful process while plastic surgeons repaired his face, but he had no duties and was able to take a university degree. Few people could have better deserved this generosity from the service, which could well have demobilised him straight away to suffer on his own. Better still, the repair was totally successful so that some years later you did not know that he had been burnt.

We had to make our own tools. Tool steel was scarce. We made chisels from skates and saws from gramophone springs, but that meant deciding whether to have a saw, or to have music. Skates were less of a problem, because there was no possibility of flooding the Sagan sand to make a rink. Brought from another camp, they were available for creating tools, but to work this sort of steel needed a file and sometimes a fire for heat treatment, but files were one thing we could not make. They had to be got by bribery, which was a job for the contact men. They were superb operators, some of whom would have won the *grand prix* at a convention of con-men.

There was one material, however, which was plentiful and needed no sophisticated tools to work it. Mild steel sheet, otherwise known as tin cans, could be cut up with ordinary scissors and rolled flat with a bottle. With the edges lapped together all sorts of things could be made, a frying pan maybe, or even a not very good blade for a bow saw. A bottle made a good enough hammer to drive in a nail so long as you hit it with the thick glass at the bottom. If the bottle broke not much was lost.

These were happy days. It was spring, and the spirit of

escape filled the air. We were busy, and I was also learning to tap dance in the chorus of a new show being produced by Vivian Kelly. The only trouble was that Lorne and I were not making much progress towards our own escape.

Then suddenly out of the blue came our big chance.

CHAPTER SIX

The Delousing Party

The Plan

ONE afternoon in April 1943 a messenger from Bushell, a 'Little X', told me that X wanted to see me at three o'clock that afternoon. I was puzzled by this summons. It could scarcely be like that ominous call to see the Station Commander at Peterborough, but what on earth could he want? When I arrived at the appointed place I found, to my surprise, not only Lorne, but a dozen others who seemed to have nothing in common to explain the gathering. Then Bushell arrived and without ado calmly announced that he had got us together because he intended to march us out through the gate. Wonders would never cease, but why me? Maybe it was all a mistake (awful thought) and I was not supposed to be there at all. But no, it was true. Lorne did not seem at all surprised, but it was not until later that I found out why.

The scheme which Bushell now outlined in clear and precise terms, like counsel presenting his case to the court, involved a party marching out of the camp in the charge of two false guards. These guards would have to wear Luftwaffe uniforms, but once outside they would discard them because they wanted civilian clothes. Reflecting on this waste of good escaping kit Bushell recalled a conversation with Lorne back in the old compound when they had discussed his ideas for flying out of Germany. That was a job for which German uniform would be essential and so he offered him a place on the scheme and asked who he would like to go with him and take the second uniform. Lorne said: "Morison." But like the good Kriegie he was he had kept the news to himself. Quite suddenly our world had turned inside out, and we knew that soon we could be outside the wire and free to make whatever was possible out of this still almost unbelievable bit of good luck.

Now the time for daydreams was over and we had to think long and hard about exactly what we would do once we were out on our own. In an attempt to start a logical analysis of how to escape, Lorne had once enunciated a basic premise: "In order to escape you have to go over the wire, under the wire, or through the wire." That may seem absurdly simplistic, but it was true and it wasn't a bad starting point from which to pursue the reasoning, which went on to say that the easiest way through a fence is through the gate—if it could be arranged. It was a big if, but Bushell's Delousing Party had solved the problem brilliantly. It was a flawless gem of escape planning and probably the most sophisticated ever in the subtlety of its design and economy of scarce resources to get the maximum number outside the wire. The reasoning behind it was as follows:

(i) To go through the gate you need German uniforms and several passes, which would be costly in escape effort. The benefit would be multiplied many-fold if Kriegies posing as guards could take a party of prisoners out with them.

(ii) The Germans will avoid moving prisoners outside the wire if they possibly can.

(iii) The only known reason for moving prisoners outside the wire is for delousing.

Lice carry typhus, a deadly disease in those days and endemic in eastern Europe. The Germans were rightly scared of it and would instantly delouse everyone in a hut where lice were discovered. Fortunately, this was rare because our hygiene was good, but it did sometimes happen. Delousing involved our clothes and bedding being baked in gigantic steam ovens, while we had a very welcome hot shower. The only delousing plant was in the *Vorlager* to the old compound and this was the vital key to the scheme, for to reach it you had to go right outside the camp and along about a hundred yards of public road (see plan on p. 100). On one side of the road was the wire, but on the other was dense fir forest into which, hopefully, we would melt. A bonus was that most of us would be able to carry our civilian clothes in our bundle of blankets, while Lorne and I would carry the clothes which we would swap for the guards' uniforms once we were safely in the woods.

X decided to discover a louse.

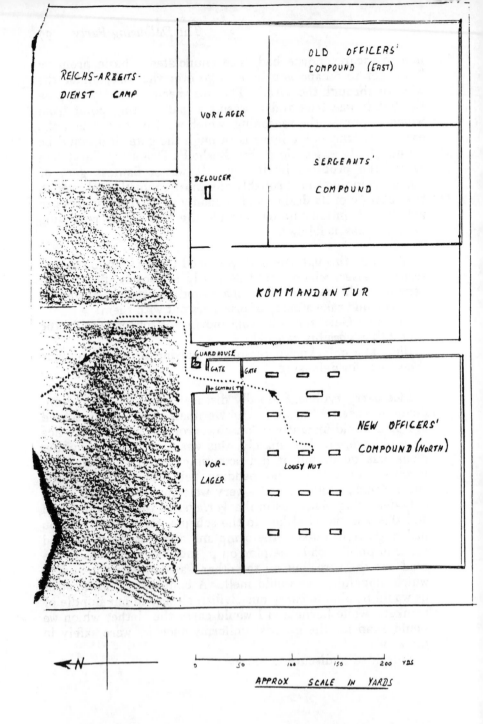

Plan of Stalag Luft III. (Drawn by Lorne Welch in 1945.)

Our Preparations

We were now pregnant with the awful secret that within two months we would walk out through the gate, but a secret it had to remain; and although our life had suddenly changed it had to appear to go on as before. We weren't needed to work on the scheme itself, so we carried on as usual with the Gadget Factory and tap dancing and all the usual activities. I was never going to appear in that show, but I could not say so. I just had to go on rehearsing; anyway, an hour's dancing and high kicks every morning was good exercise. Very discreetly Lorne and I had to get on with planning every detail of what we were belatedly recognising as the formidable task of stealing an aircraft from the Luftwaffe and flying away. For this there were some basic decisions which we had to make:

What sort of aircraft should we aim for?

Where would we find it?

What should be our destination?

Amazingly, we had in the camp detailed handling notes for the Junkers 87 and 88 bombers, that ubiquitous three engined heavy transport, the Junkers 52, the front line fighters Messerschmitt 109 and 110 and the Bucker Jungman and Jungmeister trainers. It was great to think of tearing off in a Me 110, but that was the stuff of daydreams, now no longer allowed. Such aircraft were too complicated to master in the few moments likely to be available to us, so it had to be something like the simple Buckers. Nevertheless, we memorised all we could about all the aircraft and made notes and sketches of cockpit layouts on the back of our air maps.

The destination decision was easy. England was just another daydream, as 600 miles was well out of range of a light aircraft and there would be heavily defended areas to cross. Switzerland was dismissed. It was 400 miles and the navigation would be none too easy. The only answer was Sweden, 280 miles, with the river Oder to help navigation and no heavily defended areas to cross. (See map, p. 107.) Just possibly we might have headed south towards the Balkans and Partisan country, but only if a howling northerly wind put Sweden firmly out of range. Sweden was the choice and we prepared maps for that route only. Even in still air Sweden was near the range limit of a Jungman, so I kept a meteorological record, not that it gave me much comfort.

We knew we would have very little time. The number of people out would constitute a *'Massenflucht'* (mass escape),

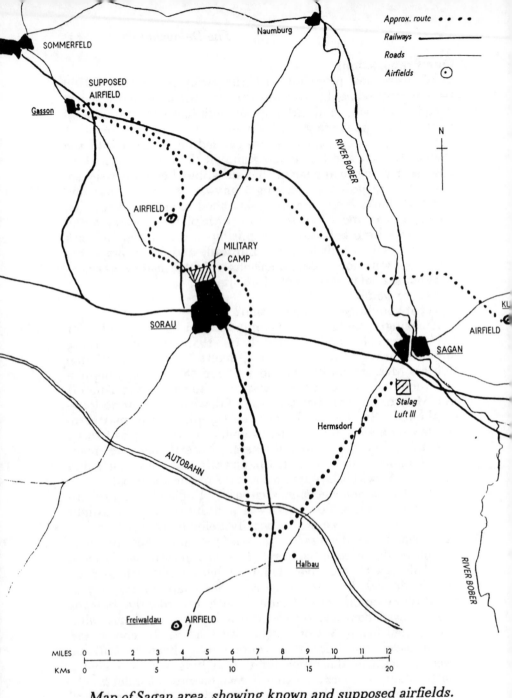

Map of Sagan area, showing known and supposed airfields.
(Reproduced from an escape map made in Stalag Luft III.)

which would instantly launch special precautions, with police and military for hundreds of miles around alerted. There would be intensive security on railway stations, ports and frontiers, so we had to get to the nearest suitable airfield and seize the first opportunity. "Sweden for dinner" became our watchword, for we reckoned that if we did not get away on the first day it would be dinner, if any, back in the cooler.

There were several possible airfields, although X's intelligence department did not have much detail. Kupper, only five miles north east of the camp, had been visited by two escapers. Its precise position was known and a sketch map of the layout was available, but to reach it we would have to pass through Sagan town, which was sure to be seething with police. Anyway, our observations of aircraft movements showed that it was mainly used by heavy aircraft, so by and large it did not seem a good proposition. At Sorau, eight miles to the west, an airfield had been spotted by a Kriegie passing in a train, but he could not give its exact position, and anyway it was too far for a first choice. At Sprottau, ten miles to the east, an airfield under construction, but already in use, was reported by a Frenchman whom someone had met in hospital. The probable confusion prevailing on a building site sounded attractive, but it was too far and the information was not over reliable. At Halbau, six miles south west and at Gasson, seventeen miles north west, escapers reported seeing light aircraft doing circuits and bumps, although they had not seen the actual fields, which in both cases were just out of their sight.

Of all this selection provided by X, Halbau sounded the most attractive, as it had the right sort of aircraft and was a flying school. There would be plenty of aircraft movement, while strange faces would be less conspicuous than on a station with a more permanent population; moreover, it was near by and could be reached without going through the town. We questioned the people who had been there, and found that two months earlier they had lain up near Halbau and had seen the aircraft passing over all day and apparently doing circuits and bumps just beyond the skyline. They had taken a compass bearing on the supposed position but couldn't pin point it exactly because they had left the camp in a hurry without accurate maps. However, when we showed them a large scale map they seemed fairly certain where they had been, and according to the map the position for the airfield was the only practicable terrain for miles around. So we chose Halbau, though not without some misgivings. There was uncertainty as to its exact position, but it was so near and accessible that it offered the best chance of getting away before the hue and cry hotted up. "Sweden for dinner" kept ringing in our ears.

In what now seemed a long time ago, when daydreaming was still allowed, there had been plenty of pessimists who said we were mad; we would never get airborne, or we would be shot down. Our reasoning was that the classic escape involved a journey of hundreds of miles on foot or by train, at the end of which—if you got that far—you had to cross a heavily guarded frontier, or stow away on a ship for Sweden. True, both had been achieved, but for every success there were a hundred failures. By contrast our 'frontier' was only six miles away at Halbau, and once airborne we would be back in our element. Flak or fighters there might be, but that would be nothing new and, anyway, we doubted whether anyone would realise that an aircraft had been stolen before we were sitting down to dinner in Sweden.

We visualised the scene if such a thing had happened back home and it went like this:

Pilot to Flight Sergeant: 'Flight, what's happened to my aircraft?'

Flight Sergeant: 'Don't know, Sir. We refuelled it half an hour ago.'

Pilot goes to Flight Office: 'Anyone know what's happened to my aircraft, H-Harry? It seems to have disappeared.'

All: 'No idea, old boy. Why don't you look after it properly? You'd better ring Ops.'

Pilot: 'Is that Ops? Do you know what's happened to my aircraft, H-Harry? It seems to have disappeared.'

Ops: 'H-Harry? Wait a minute. Yes, it took off at 15-23.'

Pilot: 'Well, who the hell—?'

And so on, but by this time H-Harry is a hundred miles away, in what direction nobody knows, and in eastern Germany there cannot have been much radar cover. Yes, it was "Sweden for dinner" alright.

That was the theory, but we still had a vast number of practical matters to deal with:

We would need food in case we were neither in Sweden, nor in the cooler for a few days, but we could not conceal much about our persons if we were to look properly dressed.

We each took three cakes of the special escaping ration whose recipe appears below, also a six ounce bar of chocolate and quarter of a pound of oatmeal, which I was sure was what had sustained my Highland ancestors when they went marauding. We made brassières to carry all this under our shirts. It was supposed to last for five days and although it sounds sickly, it was not.

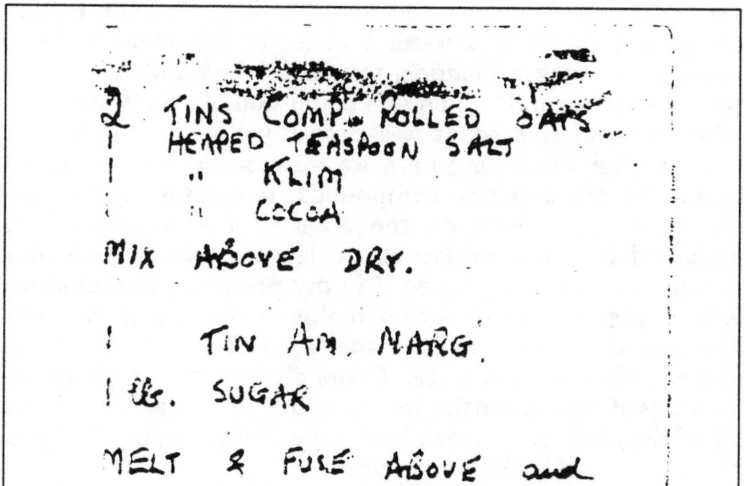

2 TINS COMP. ROLLED OATS
1 HEAPED TEASPOON SALT
1 " KLIM
   " COCOA

MIX ABOVE DRY.

1 TIN AM. MARG.
1 lb. SUGAR

MELT & FUSE ABOVE and
POUR INTO DRY MIXTURE
& WORK WITH HANDS, ADDING
AS MUCH WATER AS NECESSARY
TO MAKE IT WORKABLE —
MOULD INTO BLOCK & BAKE
SLOWLY.

DON'T BASH.

Recipe for concentrated escape rations.
(From the papers of the late Colin Dilly.)

We would have to drink, unless of course we were in Sweden for dinner, but we did not rely on that and nor could we rely on finding a convenient river every time we felt thirsty. Fortunately, Lorne had read all the World War I escaping books and remembered the story of a man who aimed to swim across the Rhine, but was't much of a swimmer and so carried a football bladder as a flotation bag. He never reached the river, but he suffered acutely from thirst because it had never occurred to him that the bladder could have doubled as a water bottle. It did occur to Lorne though, so we took a bladder, to which I had added a funnel-shaped spout through which you could pour in the water.

The origin of this spout was typically Kriegie: I saw it in the hut in the *Vorlager* where we were searched on our way between the old and new compounds. It caught my eye as a shiny aluminium knob on the door of a stove so, on the principle that it was preferable to leave a search with more than you entered it, I popped it in my pocket. An aluminium doorknob may not seem very valuable at first sight, but after I had cut the front off it made a perfect funnel for the bladder. We also took a Red Cross cheese tin, which we had been advised was essential for scooping up water—and it was good advice, too, as you can look very foolish trying to lap up water from a half-inch deep puddle.

We had the standard large scale local map which was printed in the camp from jellies and we had a flying map which the map department had constructed for us from several small scale maps, on a scale of 1:500,000 (about eight miles to the inch). It was not very accurate, but the main navigational features, the River Oder and the coastlines, were reliable, and Lorne modified it for ease of navigation by marking distances along the route and by drawing lines parallel to the track to show the distances off course. (See p. 107.) We disputed at length whether to use mph, as in RAF aircraft, or kilometres per hour, but Lorne won with the argument that the airspeed indicator was sure to be in metric.

To use a map you need a compass and so for ground work we took the standard camp pattern, which was made by moulding a piece of hot gramophone record round a glass disc. The directional needle was made from a razor blade, which could be magnetized, while the pivot was a gramophone needle, which fortunately was non-magnetic.

We were persuaded that lock picking would be a useful

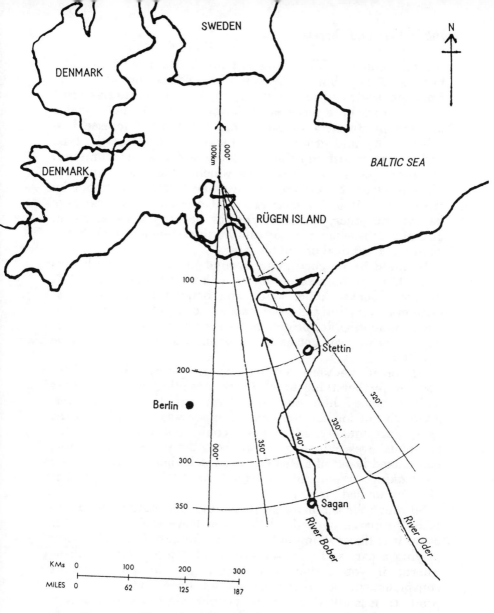

Simplified version of the Air Navigation Map designed by Lorne
Welch. The course was from Sagan to Rügen Island on the Baltic
coast, and thence to Sweden. The lines diverging from Rügen were
to help calculate course corrections. The transverse lines show the
distance still to cover to Rügen.

The River Oder, the Baltic coast and Rügen would have been
conspicuous landmarks, but the course could have been disastrous
because, as we now know, it passed over the V1 and V2 research
establishment at Peenemünde.

accomplishment. There was not much demand for opening locks at Sagan, but the person who sold us this idea came from the castle at Rothenburg and was a lock enthusiast, so I went to work on a piece of thick wire with a hammer and a file and produced a simple pick. Little did I foresee how valuable it would prove, or how lucky we were that the type and size were just right for the locks which we encountered. We also took a jemmy with us which I had made out of a piece of concrete reinforcing bar, kindly left lying about by the Goons. It had a screwdriver at one end and a carriage key at the other, useful maybe for opening a panel on an aircraft. It seemed a handy and harmless enough tool, but it caused a great deal of trouble later.

It would be no good going around unshaven, or with torn clothes, so we took razors and needle and thread, as well as matches, pocket knife, watch and handkerchief. For most escapers everything carried needed to be of German, or at least unidentifiable, origin, but we were not worried by this because if we ever got as far as being searched we would be done for.

All in all we were comprehensively equipped, but there was one further thing which Lorne's reading of escape books had convinced him we must have, and that was pepper, although not for consumption. Pepper was forbidden in the camp, presumably so that we could not throw it in the Germans' eyes, but we got a tin from the parcels officer, who had nicked it out of a Red Cross parcel when the Goons were not looking. We might just as well have taken curry powder, of which we had plenty.

So much for the material items, but our state of mind had to be prepared as well. When you leave the shelter of the camp it is like walking onto a stage. You are indeed an actor playing a part and you step into a relentlessly moving scene where, if you forget your lines, you at once become conspicuous; but there are no set lines and there is no prompt; it is all *ad lib*. Some people said it was pointless to try to prepare for every eventuality, but we preferred to practice by imagining the scene from every angle, again and again, so that when we got there it might seem familiar. Along with "Sweden for dinner" our watchword was: "Visualise the scene", and we had to make do with this as our only form of rehearsal.

When we got out we would not only be taking the guards'

uniforms, but their identity papers also, the names on which would be German. We spoke very little German, so we decided that if questioned we would say we were from Posen, a town which was in Poland in 1939, and although it was now part of Germany most of the people there spoke Polish. Not that we could speak Polish, but then nor could most Germans. We used to sit out in the compound as far as we could from other people, usually about twenty yards, and ask each other questions as to who we were and what we were doing, to which we replied in very bad German. We tried to improve our German a bit and spent roll calls, which lasted half an hour twice a day, with a well known conversation primer, but its style was typified by the phrase: "Formerly he smoked a great deal too much."—which so annoyed us that we threw it away and compiled our own selection of suitable phrases and technical aircraft terms which we gleaned from illustrated papers, dictionaries and Kriegie linguists.

Quite apart from the language problem it was difficult to think of a reason for two airmen taking an afternoon walk in the depths of the country. The best we could come up with was that we were going to visit girlfriends in the village of Kunau (wishful thinking maybe), rather than that we were searching for escaped prisoners of war, although the latter now looks the more plausible.

We also had to plan another scenario should we fail to contact our 'guards' once we were out and not get hold of the Luftwaffe uniforms. In that event we would have to go on as civilians, and for this the clothing department, although very busy, found us some simple kit, including a cap for Lorne, which fortunately he never had to wear as it made him look villainous. In this eventuality we would have no papers and our story was going to be that we were Romanians who were working in a local furniture factory and had left our papers behind. (Virtually no one outside Romania could be expected to speak Romanian.) We were just honest Romanians who wished to work for the Reich.

'Yes, indeed we work at Holzapfel's furniture factory at Eckersdorf.' (We had seen the nameplate on our lockers in the camp.) 'We have a holiday and came for a walk. Yes, certainly we have papers, but they are in our lodgings. No, we are Romanians, come here to work for the Reich.'

Obviously a weak story, but better than nothing.

We did our best to get sunburned, because if it was hot

German troops stripped off when working and we didn't want to be the only white skins in sight. We studied German magazines for scenes of life on aerodromes and we tramped round the 'circuit' in boots to get in training for what might be a long walk. In the camp, 'Come and do a circuit' was not only for the exercise; it was also a social invitation. It was the only sure way of getting enough distance from the next man to have a private conversation, and as such it was ideal for visualising a scene which had to remain secret. When some new idea needed discussion there were worse things to do than a quick circuit after we had packed up the Gadget Factory in the evening. In the dusk, before the perimeter lights were switched on and we were shut up in our huts for the night, the uglier features of the landscape faded from view. The huts, the wire and the people could be forgotten and if you were lucky you might arrive back, lean in the window of your room and be given a cup of cocoa. The wilting tomato plants would look almost healthy in the cool of a May evening and the pine trees, dark and drab in winter, spread their scent over the camp.

The date of departure was put back several times so we were getting over-rehearsed. Sometimes tempers became frayed, but life was pleasant enough. The choice of room mates had proved fortunate and we lived peacefully, often hilariously, although it must have been about now that Lorne produced one of his least hilarious, but most memorable remarks. The lights were out, we had all gone to bed and we were playing 'Knock Knock'.
Lorne: "Knock knock."
All: "Who's there?"
Lorne: "Focke Wulf." (A Luftwaffe single seat fighter.)
All (puzzled): "Focke Wulf who?"
Lorne: "Focke Wulf in the dark."
Dead silence. Total mystification. It was too late to try and puzzle this one out, so we all went to sleep.
If an evening circuit was agreeable then so it was to lie in bed in the morning while Nick Pollock, who had a passion for early rising, brought breakfast. Nick was distinguished by having received a telephone call a few minutes after landing by parachute in Denmark. He had taken refuge in a farm house and had only been there a few minutes when the phone rang. The farmer lifted the receiver, listened for a moment,

then said: "It's for you," and handed it to Nick. It turned out to be one of his crew who had gone to another farm nearby, but alas! they were both soon picked up by the Germans. Nick was also distinguished by being the owner of the twelve stringed lute and by the conviction that when he got home he would land at Leith, but his happiest traits were his early rising and his tendency to leave the lute hanging on the wall, where it made a better show as decoration than as a musical instrument in his hands.

Preparation of the scheme itself was far more complex than the bare idea may suggest. People had walked out through gates before and the Germans had created formidable defences. Two fluent German speakers were required as guards; they were Roger de Wever, a Belgian, and a Dutch Pilot Officer, Geesink. Both had to be equipped not only with German uniforms, but with false papers. The documents required were the ordinary soldier's pay book, which also served as an identity card and to which the camp's security officer had added a page with a photograph of the holder. Then a pass was required by any German entering the prisoners' compound and finally a special pass, issued only in exceptional circumstances to authorise a particular prisoner, or party, to be taken outside the wire. The first two documents were produced by draughtsmen painstakingly working with pen and ink and were indistinguishable from the real thing, while the blank forms of the special pass were obtained by bribery. Just how this formidable feat was performed we did not know and did not ask. Our business was installing tunnel ventilation and we didn't expect other people to ask how we did it. These special passes were issued by the Goon security officer himself and one can only wonder at the power of persuasion which procured the blanks and at the guards who would risk almost certainly being shot for handing them over.

The uniforms were rather easier, the tunics being made from airmen's great coats which we got from the Red Cross, the colour of which was similar to that of the Luftwaffe although a little powder was needed to adjust the tone. Most of the badges and insignia, leather belts, holsters and so on had to be got by bribery, although we made some buttons by melting silver paper into moulds of soap. I was worried that the cloth looked so new and that no one seemed interested in ageing it, despite the fact that you never saw a Goon in a new uniform. However, time and again the outfits passed inspection at only a few feet so evidently I was wrong.

The actual passage out through the gate was going to need very precise organisation and timing. Two genuine guards would come into the compound to collect us, but it was necessary that the sentries on the gate should change before we tried to go out, as otherwise it was likely that they would notice different faces going out from those who came in. It was therefore arranged that a normal party would go to the delouser in the morning, and we said that the second (escaping) party would be ready after lunch, at a time which we chose to be just after the gate sentries' change was due. When the real guards came in they would be diverted by the offer of coffee and cigarettes, and then as soon as the sentries changed we would be off. There was ample opportunity for something to foul up and land us all straight in the cooler, or at best require aborting before we got under way, but Bushell's planning was meticulous and hopefully Murphy's Law was in suspense.

Although we were fully occupied with visualising the scene and all the other preparations we still found time to wonder what would happen if we were caught, as it was obvious that we would have quite a lot to laugh off. The Goons had recently issued an order which forbade the wearing of German uniform or civilian clothes outside the camp and rendered those doing so liable to court martial on charges of espionage or sabotage. Civilian clothes had always been worn (how could you escape without?), so either this was a serious breach of the rules or, as we hoped, they did not really mean it. But German uniform was just what we were going to wear, and worse still we were going to try and nick a Luftwaffe aircraft, which sounded distinctly like sabotage. It did not pay to visualise this particular scene too closely, so we tried to forget it.

The Gleam of Sweden in a Kriegie's Eye

By the first week of June we were ready. We had tried on the German uniforms and they fitted. Our compass was buried in the garden. Our maps were in the Gadget Factory's tool hide and our food rations were doing their best to look innocent among the normal stores in our food cupboard.

It was said that you could tell a Kriegie who was about to escape by the 'Gleam of Sweden' in his eye, and by now our room mates had recognised the signs. They knew we were about to leave them, but knew nothing of the Delousing Party, supposing that we were bound for the tunnel whose ventilation system we had been working on. We had already installed the pumps in Tom, Dick and Harry and Lorne had moved on to designing a railway system to evacuate the sand, though we knew that we would never finish it. Lorne had chosen Jens Muller to take over the Gadget Factory but could not tell him until the last minute, while I kept rehearsing for the show in which I would not appear.

On 9 June Bushell called us to a final briefing. We assembled in an empty room where in addition to the members of the Delousing Party there was a small group composed of senior officers. It turned out that there was a spare copy of the special group pass and rather than waste it Bushell had organised this party to follow us out, using the excuse that they were going to an interview with the Kommandant. The atmosphere was reminiscent of the ops room at Elsham Wolds almost exactly a year before. That briefing had landed me in captivity and now this one, which was no less tense, would maybe get me out. Bushell was in his element as he issued his final instructions. Months of planning were coming to fruition and he seemed to take a delight in his role as Big X, master-minding the escaping organisation. He gave out some last items of equipment: money, German matches, maps and, most important, the various papers which would be needed by those travelling overland, most of them by train. Only one thing was held back and that was the precious set of gate passes.

We were told that next morning, if the show was still on, we would be invited to 'a game of roulette'—another touch of cloak and dagger, but necessary none the less. Then we went out into the warm, still June evening: Wing Commanders, Pilot Officers and Colonels; a fighter ace, a pilot shot down on his first trip; English, Belgian, American, Dutch— all looking no doubt like ordinary Kriegies, but each about to give birth to the secret scheme with which we had become pregnant two months previously.

The next morning—10 June—dawned fine, and we hung about our room anxiously waiting for the invitation to roulette, until at last the messenger arrived. Lorne went off to warn Jens to take over the Gadget Factory as he would be busy elsewhere for a few days, while I apologised to my dancing master, saying that I had an urgent engagement. Our room mates were envious that we were off. We told them to keep at the opposite corner from the gate in case their curiosity got the better of their discretion, while the Little X in our hut advised them to get down on their knees and pray if they heard a trumpet. A trumpet blast was to be the warning if shooting became imminent.

We had lunch, but were too excited to eat much. Then, as we dressed, there was a brief moment of farce when Lorne found a vital trouser button was missing.

"I've got a bachelor button," said Nick Pollock.

"Well, can I have it?" asked Lorne.

"Yes. If you return it later."

Anyway, there was no time for sewing so Lorne fixed the bachelor button. They all wished us good luck and we walked off towards the assembly hut, carrying our bundles of bedding and trying to look inconspicuous. Meanwhile the wheels of the elaborate escape machine had begun to turn in earnest. The clothing department had brought the uniforms and were dressing the guards. The man from 'Dean & Dawson' (a leading pre-war travel agency and the name given to our forgery den) was standing by with the passes, waiting to date stamp them when it was certain that we would go. In the middle of the camp an open air debate on trial marriage was getting under way so as to keep as many as possible of the unemployed innocently occupied, while as a further pre-caution the approaches to the gate were being unobtrusively patrolled to prevent a crowd of onlookers from gathering. Somewhere the trumpeter waited, watching the Goon Box which overlooked the road and ready to sound the blast which would send us diving for the cover of the trees if the Goon raised his rifle. But that particular Goon was supposed to be watching a fencing match at a spot where his gaze could safely fall.

The escapers themselves sat nursing their nerves in the hut, but among us were two very different sets of people, for that morning, to Bushell's horror, the Germans had started taking parties of twenty four instead of fifteen and he had had to find and equip nine people to escape at a few hours' notice. Some of us were prepared in every detail, while the others were still breathlessly gathering themselves together.

Then it suddenly emerged that one small, but potentially disastrous bit of preparation had gone wrong: I was looking at the pay book which was to become Lorne's and saw that it was in the name of *Obergefreiter* (Corporal) Knopp. A shiver ran through me as I looked up at Knopp and, yes, I thought so, he wore only the single chevron of a *Gefreiter*. The tailors found another stripe and we all held our breath while anxious fingers sewed it on. Then the crisis passed and once again time dragged. It was hot, and one very tough Kriegie turned pale and asked for a drink of water. People laughed nervously at bad jokes, rumour abounded—perhaps something had miscarried, perhaps it would be put off for today, perhaps then for weeks. We had been waiting too long at the end of the runway for the green light and maybe the 'Gleam of Sweden' was beginning to fade.

Then suddenly the green light flashed and we were off, trooping out into the bright sunshine, a typical party of Kriegies, shambling and slightly truculent.

CHAPTER SEVEN

To the Airport

ONCE again, just as though we were rolling down the runway bound for the Ruhr, we were gripped by the inevitable unfolding of events from which there was now no turning back. Roger de Wever, at the front of the column, reached the first gate and we held our breath. There was a delay and some words were exchanged. Maybe the sentry was suspicious. But then one of the senior officers in the party waiting behind us shouted some abuse:

"What the hell is going on? We'll be late for the Kommandant. Get a move on there!"

That authoritative military voice did the trick and the guard let us through. Then came the second gate, but this time there was no hold up and suddenly we were out—out, but still in view, and the warning trumpet could still have sent us scurrying for cover.

It was crucial that the road should be clear, but it wasn't. An ox cart was coming towards us. The driver looked lke a Pole, but all the same we dawdled, waiting for him to pass. Our 'guards' shouted at us to keep moving and we cursed back at them. It was a typical scene, but we could not delay too long or we would hold up the senior officers' party, so we melted away into the trees and for the moment at least we were free.

A minute later an extraordinary scene unfolded in the woods as twenty four prisoners were transformed into businessmen, commercial travellers and workmen, who vanished as quickly as they had come, leaving only piles of discarded clothing. Meanwhile, I had transformed myself into a Luftwaffe *Gefreiter* and was shouting in a stage whisper for Lorne, whom I had lost in the excitement. I couldn't see him so, deciding that it was time I left this unhealthy neighbourhood, I set off along our intended route, expecting to find him doing the same. It was a bit unnerving, but after a few hundred yards I saw a Luftwaffe man coming up behind me. There were some moments of mutual anxiety in case the other were the real thing, but all was well and with high hopes Lorne and I headed for Halbau and home.

Back at the camp things were not going so well. The senior officers had been caught out between the gates, but while the Goons were haranguing them on the futility of trying to escape the news came that twenty six prisoners had disappeared on the way to the delouser and the air of smug satisfaction melted from their faces.

Nor were things going well on Sagan railway station, where many of the escapers were waiting for the Berlin express, which they hoped would get them away from the area before the search warmed up. By ill fortune a German officer from the camp chanced to be on the platform and recognised one of the Kriegies, so that in minutes they were all rounded up and returned to the cooler, almost before they had started. This really set the alarm bells ringing. The hunt was on at full blast and was so successful that within two days the only ones still out were three who, while the round-up was proceeding at the station, were walking down the road to Halbau. The third was a 'workman' whom we found ourselves overtaking soon after we had left Sagan. We eyed him anxiously from behind, fearing that if we overtook him he might test our weak German by passing the time of day with us. But we pressed on and as we drew near Lorne thought he recognised him as 'one of us'. In fact it was Johnny Stower, who was hard-arsing it towards Switzerland, and as we passed we exchanged a furtive greeting.

It was the last we ever saw of Johnny, for two weeks later he was picked up near the Swiss frontier and nine months after that he was shot by the Gestapo after the mass break out from the tunnel Harry. Alas for Johnny, one of the most determined and courageous escapers, and a pilot whom Lorne had taught in his days as an instructor.

Before long we were in the village of Hermsdorf and we were getting nervous. We had been out for over an hour and the hue and cry must surely be on. There seemed to be no good reason for an *Obergefreiter* and a *Gefreiter* of the Luftwaffe to be walking along this road on a hot June afternoon, so we branched off down a track which ran parallel to the road. We passed a few people working in the fields, but they took no notice, and soon we arrived at a point from which we could overlook the area where the airfield was supposed to lie.

On the way we had seen no aerial activity. True, it was Whit Friday and a public holiday, but when we could find no

sign of an airfield either our spirits sank to the bottom. We
watched for aircraft movements for a while, but when some
three hours had passed since we had walked so hopefully
through the gates, we felt ourselves to be increasingly
exposed. It was no longer a case of risking everything with a
quick dash for an aircraft. Hundreds of people might now be
looking for us and the time had come to get out of sight. To
reach good cover meant crossing the Berlin to Breslau autobahn, but foot traffic was forbidden and to cross by a bridge
half a mile to the east invited disaster, so we lay down in the
nearest cover to think things over. It was swelteringly hot,
we had just walked eight miles, we were tired, thirsty and disappointed and we felt that we had had it. We had been
unable to fill our football bladders with water, so we drank
from a small glass bottle which we had brought for
emergencies. We rested for just five minutes, then decided
to cross the autobahn and make for woods to the west of the
railway where we could overlook the country from a new
angle and where there were forests in which to hide.

Just as we arrived at the road we were drenched by a heavy
thunderstorm. We pressed on as soon as it stopped, passing
a few houses near the road. After the storm there was no one
about and we got away into open fields where we drank
delicious muddy water from puddles, with invaluable help
from our cheese tins. Then we crossed over the railway and
back over the autobahn to a new vantage point, but still we
could not see any airfield.

It was evening now and the only thing to do was lie up. We
found a plantation of young fir trees and crawled into the
middle, but we felt far from secure, for we discovered what
we should have known already, that only dense undergrowth
gives good cover. In a wood, and particularly a fir wood,
where the canopy cuts out most of the light, there is little
undergrowth so there is clear visibility along the rows of
trees. We feared that we had made a terrible noise getting
into the wood and we could hear dogs barking not far away,
which did nothing to improve our nerves. The rain set in
steadily and it got dark. We felt small and far from home
and began to have visions of hot dinners and dry beds back in
the camp. In the RAF this sort of thing was called 'lack of
moral fibre', but at least we admitted it to one another, and
after eating our ration of escaper's compound we felt better.
We even got a drink by shaking drops of water off the leaves

into our tins, but it was an exasperatingly slow method. Every noise horrified us and we were in a permanent state of apprehension, afraid to face the open, but equally reluctant to endure much longer this wet, dark hole which seemed far from safe.

Then a little thought showed that searching for the airfield next day would be even more dangerous, so we decided to search during the night and if that failed, to lie up all the next day. We started at eleven and soon felt much better. The weather had cleared and we were doing something again. We searched until dawn, but although it was pleasantly adventurous prowling through the woods and fields by moonlight we found no airfield and we saw no people.

Came the dawn and we found a plantation to lie up in, but it was far from ideal. A casual passer by would not have seen us, but a searcher could hardly have failed. We excavated shallow graves in the sandy soil, camouflaging the newly turned sand with pine needles, and then I expended the pepper. It was hard not to feel a fool while shaking a diminutive pot of pepper all round a two acre wood—and anyway a dog would have seen us long before it started to sneeze—but at last it was done and by an hour after dawn we were ready to settle down to the hardest of all escaping jobs: lying up. We agreed that no matter how bored or restless we became we would not move until ten o'clock, when it would be dusk, and so we were faced with sixteen hours in which to do nothing.

As soon as we stopped moving about we felt cold, and we remained cold for the rest of the day. We managed to sleep for an hour or two in turn, but we were too keyed up and uncomfortable to sleep for long. A few people came past, but we saw nothing of the general search which we knew must be going on all over the area. Once or twice we heard what might have been engines being run up and one or two aircraft flew over, but there was nothing to go on. It was still the Whitsun holiday and, as it turned out, we saw almost no aircraft in the air until after Monday. We subsequently found out that there was an airfield at Freiwaldau, five miles south west of Halbau, which was presumably the one reported to us, and if normal flying had been in progress we might have found it, but as it was we decided to abandon Halbau and head for Sorau, where a Kriegie passing on a train had actually seen an airfield, although he could not exactly locate it. We now realised that our tactic must be to avoid detection until we found a suitable airfield and that therefore we must travel only at night. As dusk approached, and it seemed as if we would survive the day, we left our temporary prison and set off on the sixteen mile walk to the north.

It was a perfect June night, brilliantly moonlit, and with the exhilaration of the fresh night air and the impression of speed born of the darkness we seemed to slip effortlessly across country, along woodland paths, across fields of standing corn—it was alien corn—and past sleeping farms and villages. We found plenty of drinking water and filled the football bladder. I was always thirsty and developed a satisfying knack of drinking from the bladder while on the move. Gentle pressure brought the water welling up from where it hung under my shirt, flavoured with a delightful bouquet of rubber, mud, leaves and the minty taste peculiar to ditches.

At one point the path led us into a farm. From the shadows we emerged into a moonlit scene where tall white-washed buildings with high pitched roofs stood above a hollow surrounded by trees, for all the world like a fairy tale. Below us frogs were croaking in a mill pool, but otherwise all was silence. We paused for a moment, overawed, then climbed noisily over a fence, dropped down past the frogs, passed a village where we went through a tunnel under the railway and came again into open country. We skirmished on, pausing to read the map by match light, and flinging ourselves flat on our faces in Kunzendorf as an early cyclist passed a few yards away. We doubled our speed as dawn began to dim the moonlight when we were still a couple of miles from Sorau. It was a wonderful night's walking. The countryside was so deserted that it belonged to us alone, with mile upon mile of freedom after a year of barbed wire, barren sand and packed humanity.

Soon after dawn we reached a hillside just east of Sorau which was covered with fir trees only six feet high and gave excellent cover. We chose a spot on a ridge from which we could overlook all the country to the south, while the town itself and the country to the north were hidden by a slightly higher ridge. We were full of optimism and confident that as the day grew older we would see either the airfield, or aircraft on the circuit. The midsummer night being short, we had had to travel fast and were tired enough to go straight to sleep as soon as we had picked the best spot, but an hour later we woke wet and cold. The perfect June night had given way to rain and low cloud which looked as though it would last all day, so we built a shelter by bending together adjacent rows of trees and piling heather on top as a crude thatch. When we had piled on so much heather that our house looked ready to collapse we crawled in, and despite the cramped quarters managed to keep dry and sleep a bit.

By midday the weather had cleared, but not an aircraft did we see and nor could we see the airfield. Lorne wanted to go and look over the ridge to the north, while I argued that it was Whit Sunday afternoon and that thousands of people would be about, half of them probably looking for us. But after long debate we went, on the shaky pretext that we would stick to the woods and that sooner than meet people we would come back. Thus we broke our good resolution only to travel by night until we were on an airfield and deservedly we were at once deeply in the mire. First we passed people picking blueberries, then we nearly walked into a whole crowd while climbing a fence beside a road. Our trouble was that we were undecided whether to come out into the open or to keep out of sight. We tried both in quick succession, dithered, got distinctly panicky and scuttled into the first cover we could see, where we lay feeling like ostriches without enough sand to cover our heads. Clearly our position was bad. We were in a wood on the edge of a fair sized town on Whit Sunday afternoon while Everyman and his Girl seemed to be wandering about in it. The cover was indifferent and we could hear shots from a sporting gun and a barking dog which might well flush us out like rabbits. A soldier passed silently as a shadow only twenty yards away and we lay petrified; then, when all was quiet and a little courage had returned, we cut some bushes and planted them in the gaps, but it only improved the cover slightly and there could have been no disguising that we were hiding. We resumed our determination not to move until dark and so we lay in a permanent state of jitters for eight agonisingly long hours, attacked by mosquitoes and horseflies.

Dusk brought release at last and we set off to search to the east and north of the town. It seemed promising ground and despite parties of home-going revellers all went well. Finally we came to a high wire fence behind which were concrete roads and buildings which, although in the style of farm buildings, looked distinctly military. Then a patrol passed inside the fence—causing us heart flutter, but at least confirming that it was a military establishment. From our map it looked as though there was just room for an airfield in this area, so we crept round the fence trying to get a better view. There was some activity inside, but after spending time flat on our faces when we thought someone was looking for us with a torch we decided that prowling round a military camp in the small hours of the morning was too risky and we pushed off back to our heather house. There we decided that by this time the search would have moved further away from Sagan and that tomorrow it would be safe to move in daylight.

The day dawned painfully slowly and no sooner had the sun risen than it was obscured by cloud. With few clothes and little to eat we were cold, but then the air warmed up and we spent the morning sunbathing and doing repairs to our uniforms, which the clothing department had evidently built only for the passage through the gate. During the morning we saw Dornier 215 bombers passing over, but they were not on local flying. However, it was still Whitsun and we were sure that there must be an airfield somewhere near.

When we reached good cover such as we now had it was like going off-stage, where you can relax and let the world get on without you, but now we were faced with making another entrance. We had got used to roaming about the country, but except for the first few hours it had all been at night and secretly. Now our first full dress performance was about to start. We felt that we might look out of place walking about in the morning, but in the afternoon we sallied forth onto the road which we hoped bounded the airfield and soon we found ourselves plunging deeper and deeper into what proved to be not an airfield, but a huge army depot. It was a blazing hot afternoon and there were people everywhere, all in their Sunday best, which made us feel scruffy. The road ran right through the camp, but we could not turn back without looking odd; nor, with so many people about, could we discuss what to do next, so we just pressed on.

Happily we passed through the camp without incident and then found the road leading us down into Sorau, which was a biggish town in which we certainly did not want to get immersed. At the same moment we spotted what were almost certainly hangars and a wind sock on the skyline to the north.

An airfield at last.

But to reach it we had to make a long detour through what seemed to be the grandfather of all ribbon developments. We were hot and thirsty and had no water left. We kept passing beer gardens and were sorely tempted, but none had any customers and although we might have managed a simple *'Zwei Bier, bitte'*, we did not feel up to a solo conversation with the waiter. We trudged on until we reached the airfield, but there the prospect did not cheer us up at all. It was surrounded by a high wire fence and there was no cover anywhere near from which to observe it. There were hangars, workshops and accommodation for civilian workers which made it look like a factory. We saw Luftwaffe officers lying on the lawn of their mess sipping beer. It was a nostalgic scene and at that particular moment they seemed to be having the best of the war.

Having seen all we needed for the time being we headed for woods two miles to the north to recuperate. There were still a lot of people about and some gave us rather odd looks. Maybe it was our scruffy appearance, or the fact that we wore pistols. We had an idea that we should be wearing bayonets for walking out, but decided to hang on to the imitation pistols, which we learned later was quite wrong. So much for our efforts to 'visualise the scene'.

Once in the woods we joined in the general blueberry picking as a substitute for a drink, then found a thick patch of bracken and flopped down exhausted, not much caring what happened. Our peace was short lived for we heard a party of people shouting and banging about in the wood. They sounded like a search party, but they settled down forty yards away, laughing, joking and enjoying themselves. They didn't speak German so probably they were foreign workers, but we never saw them, so all we could do was lie still and if necessary pretend we were just a couple of airmen having an afternoon siesta, which in fact is what we were.

After an hour they went away, but soon a fresh trial appeared in the shape of rain. We built a shelter of saplings and bracken which worked for half an hour, but soon it became saturated and we quickly followed its example. As ever we were thirsty, but once again we collected water by shaking leaves into our tins. Maybe we collected a tin full each, but it was an agonising business waiting until there was enough in the tin to actually taste. I was determined that the first task for the night should be to find a sufficient supply of water before we set out on a further reconnaisance of the airfield, and I remembered a notice by a stream which we had passed in the ribbon development village which was headed 'Löschwasser' in large letters. I didn't know what that meant, but as it was followed by dire warnings against chuting rubbish, or otherwise polluting, I took it for drinking water. Subsequently we saw several such notices over water which looked far from drinkable, which is not surprising as the word means water for fire extinguishing. Not that that would have deterred us as we drank from puddles, ditches and rivers downstream of large towns and never felt any ill effects.

As soon as it was dark we set off for this *Löschwasser*, although it was two miles away. The route took us past the north side of the airfield at which point we saw a gigantic black cloud bearing down on us from behind. A first class thunderstorm was about to break, so we scuttled back to a Dutch barn which we had just passed. As we arrived the storm enveloped us in total darkness and streaming rain, but we were safely in the dry and the drinking problem was solved by the puddles which soon formed. The barn was only a hundred yards from the airfield and was full of straw almost to the roof, so we were not only in the dry, but from the top of the straw we would have a splendid observation post when daylight returned. There was now no point in going on with our reconnaissance so we took off our wet tunics, buried ourselves in the straw and went to sleep.

I did not wake until eight o'clock the next morning, and when I did it was dark, or so it seemed, but Lorne said he had been watching the airfield and had seen some Focke-Wulf 190s, including one only just inside the fence. I found that I had sunk six feet down in the straw, which explained the darkness, so I scrambled up and took my turn at watching through a knot hole. It was a tedious job and revealed only an occasional 190 doing test flights, while from time to time the aircraft inside the fence, which was chocked up in the butts, fired its guns with a devastating roar, which was bad for the nerves. The evidence suggested that this was a Focke-Wulf assembly plant, but as the 190 was a sophisticated single seater fighter, and as we saw no other aircraft activity, we wrote the place off as useless for our purpose.

To make the day as unpleasant as possible some farm workers came into the barn for lunch and although we could not see them we judged that some of them spent the afternoon there asleep. Anyway we were taking no risks, and lay as still as possible to prevent the straw from rustling. Straw is far from windproof and chilly draughts blew through it to add to our discomfort. When at last evening came we thought there might still be someone down below, but all was well, and for the first time in eight hours we had the luxury of being able to move more than an inch at a time.

We were hungry, but had precious little food left. However, during the day we had seen a pigeon flying in and out, and as it was nesting time Lorne went searching for pigeons' eggs and found two. I cut the top off one and sucked out the contents, but perhaps it was a bit too late in the nesting season because there was a bony sort of consistency about it, and although it was nearly dark Lorne must have seen my face, because he refused to eat his.

We had plenty of time during the day to plan our next move. Sorau was evidently a washout and the only remaining choices were Kupper or Gasson. Kupper was only a few miles from the camp. We knew its position, but we also knew that it was used mostly by big bombers and that to reach it we would have to pass through Sagan town, which we did not fancy. Gasson was another of those airports reported by an escaper who had watched aircraft doing circuits and bumps, but had not seen the actual field. However, they were light aircraft, which was what we wanted, and wittingly—but maybe foolishly—we chose Gasson and set off through the night for what turned out to be another phantom airfield. We never saw it and even though the Whitsun hoilday was over we sw no aircraft other than birds of passage. We were now short of food and becoming exhausted. Morale sank low, although there was a small moment of triumph when we achieved our first conversation in German. A Pole working in a field greeted is with: *"Gehen sie spazieren?"* ("Are you going for a walk?") To which Lorne made the masterly reply: *"Ja. Schön, nicht wahr?"* ("Yes. Lovely isn't it?")

Not that it did my moral much good, because I was supposed to be the one who could speak German.

So it was back to Kupper, back almost into the jaws of Stalag Luft III, but by now we had no alternative. Sorau to Gasson had taken us further away from Sagan so that we were faced by a walk of more than twenty miles. We only had half a day's food left, but we reckoned we could make it if we

walked directly along the main road by night—and hang the
consequences. We were well off our large scale local map so
we went into the town to look for sign posts. The first shock
was to find ourselves marching along fifty yards in front of a
Hitler Youth Band, badly out of step despite the music; then
we found that the only road went through Sorau, a town
which we had no wish to pass through again, and finally we
were driven almost mad by smells of cooking which wafted
across the road.

If the night walk from Halbau to Sorau had been a
highlight of my life then the walk to Kupper was a rock
bottom low. Our old enemy the thunderstorm caught us in
the evening, but we were lucky to find a tool shed in the
middle of a field whose lock yielded to Lorne's skill with the
pick. There we spent a dry night, which I passed in a semi-
nightmare, half-waking in the black darkness and wondering
where I was. Fatigue was beginning to tell. In the morning
we went on, not in fact on the main road, but following small
roads and paths roughly parallel to the railway. The trouble
with these country roads was that the villages were strung
out along them almost continuously so that we were always
visible. Every farm had a milk churn outside waiting for
collection, and although we desperately needed food we could
scarcely rob the churns in full view of the houses. In one
village we saw a notice board with the legend: *'Hier spricht
die NSDAP'* ('Nazi Party Notices'), and were encouraged to
see nothing on it about a reward for the capture of escaped
prisoners; but it could easily have been otherwise for two
days earlier we had been featured in a special edition of the
German 'Criminal Police Gazette'.

Prisoners of war, other than officers, were extensively
employed outside their camps on working parties, of which
we saw several along our way, but unfortunately none of them
were British. Had they been we might have got some food
because these parties were often very loosely supervised. We
might have had some difficulty establishing our bona fides
but the tactics employed by another British officer in the
same situation could have worked for us. Although dressed
as a *Feldwebel* he approached an English soldier working in a
field and said fiercely: *"Sind Sie ein Englander?"* and when
the reply was *"Ja,"* he said in a strong London accent:
"That's orl right mate, so am I."

We trudged on towards Kupper, downhearted and feeling

that we had made a mess of our big chance. The day was hot
and our legs were reluctant. We got badly tied up in a wood
where none of the paths led in the right direction, but in
spite of everything we made fair progress and early in the
afternoon reached the River Bober. We were still not on the
large scale local map for the Sagan area, but we knew that we
had to cross the river and so all we had to do was to follow the
bank until we reached a bridge. First, however, we treated
ourselves to an hour's rest on a secluded promontory in the
stream. We fancied a swim, but reckoned we couldn't risk
getting caught without our trousers, so we made do with a
good drink and a foot bath. It was so peaceful by the river
that we did not want to move, but when at last we persuaded
our creaking muscles to hoist us on to the road again we felt
a lot better, and after a couple of hours we were on the local
map again at Bargisdorf, where there was a bridge. We had
another brief rest by the river and sampled the water, but it
tasted of Sagan. However, we were lucky to find a little fresh
stream a bit further on, where we filled up.

To reach Kupper we followed the main road for a mile and
then cut across country, but progress was becoming painfully
slow because I at least was finding every possible excuse to
stop, even for a minute. We had eaten our last small piece of
chocolate early in the morning, and from now on every bit of
energy had to be scraped up from the bottom of a none too
accessible store which the masses of blueberries we found did
little to replenish, although they were refreshing. By now it
was late afternoon and once again the thunderstorms were
building up. We were reluctant to get wet, not only because
of comfort, but because we could not afford to look
bedraggled. During one heavy shower we sheltered near a lot
of people who had been picking blueberries, but the Germans
seemed to be almost waterproof, and when the rain eased
they started for home while we stuck to our tree, miserable
with the thought that we were letting down the Luftwaffe by
being softies.

About six in the evening we arrived at the airfield and at
once our spirits lifted when we saw what we had been
searching for for so long: a small biplane doing flying
practice. Maybe Kupper was not all big bombers and we
were going to be in luck. We started to explore, making a
detour round the side opposite to the hangars, which took us
through another long village where it rained yet again. It

looked as though there was plenty more rain to come, so prospects for the night were bleak until we moved off up a track where fortune found us two perfect shelters. They were haycocks beside a copse and only a few hundred yards from the airfield; they were the sort where hay is heaped over a wooden tripod to dry and it was possible to creep in underneath, where we could scarcely have been safer or more comfortable.

We had seen gates in the airfield fence. At one there was a sentry, but one near to our hide appeared to be unguarded and so at about midnight we crept out on reconnaissance. We approached the gate cautiously, but found no sign of a sentry or patrols, so out came the pick and once again the lock yielded to Lorne's gentle touch. When we were sure that we could open and shut it with reasonable certainty we withdrew to the safety of our haycocks, but now the adrenalin was flowing and we were too excited and restless to coop ourselves up for long.

There was a potato field alongside, and although the new potatoes were only the size of peas the seed potatoes from which the plants had grown were still there and we resolved to cook some. There was a gravel pit in the copse and in it we lit a fire which was invisible from outside. Into it went the seed potatoes and we waited impatiently for our first decent meal for days, but alas! they turned out a pulpy and disgusting mess, presumably because the potato gives up its store of starch to feed the growing plant. So, disappointed, we retired to bed and, pulling the hay around us, contrived to keep warm for the rest of the night.

In the morning the coast was clear and the time had come to make ourselves presentable for an appearance on the airfield. We had only brought one razor blade apiece. Goon blades were never very sharp and by now ours were hopelessly blunt; but that was not the worst, for during the night a mass of hayseeds had worked their way into our tunics and it took an hour of picking and scraping with a knife before we could think of being seen at close quarters by the beady eye of a *Feldwebel* expecting his men to be smartly turned out. Finally our clothes were as good as we could get them and we set out to enter the International Departures Lounge.

CHAPTER EIGHT

Crime and Punishment

THERE was no one in sight.

Lorne wielded the lock pick. The gate yielded, and we walked at last onto our goal, a Luftwaffe airfield. No weariness now—just excitement, for it was now or never. Just as we had always visualised the scene for Halbau, now we would have to grasp the first chance.

We were on the far side from the buildings, and a minute later, as we were walking round the perimeter track towards them, a Junkers W 34 landed, taxied up to the control tower and was left there by its crew. This looked promising. We knew no details of its handling, but it was evidently a light single engined communications aircraft with a fixed undercarriage, similar to its big brother, the familiar, and notorious, three engined Junkers 52. It was simple but substantial. It was ideal.

When we got round to the tower the Junkers was still standing a hundred and fifty yards out on the field, just waiting for us, but I took the line that as we were here we might as well take a quick look round to see whether there was anything better—and that was a mistake.

We walked on, and as we passed an NCO we saluted smartly, but he took no notice, which gave us courage. We found more W 34s laid up under some trees and tried to get in to check out the cockpits, but they were locked. Then we noticed that few of the airmen whom we saw were wearing belts, let alone side arms, so we dumped ours in the first place which offered, a goods train standing in a siding on the airfield. A funny place to put them maybe, but we were convinced that in a few minutes we would be airborne for Sweden.

Having got ourselves properly dressed we set out for the aircraft. There was no one about except for some men loading a small transport aircraft a hundred yards away; but they were not interested, so we scrambled into the passenger cabin. Out of sight we felt more secure, for if no one had remarked on our entry there would be nothing suspicious to see, at least until we started turning the engine. We were

soon in the cockpit and found an ideal set up with side-by-
side dual control, maps and ample fuel. We felt better and
better. The controls were all clear; we turned on the fuel,
pumped up the fuel pressure and doped the engine—all
routine aircraft practice. Now came the first hitch: we could
see no sign of electric starting, but an ugly great starting
handle was much in evidence and that meant getting out
again into full view to wind up by hand. That was a most
unwelcome prospect, and the vision of the Swedish coast
which had been coming up over the horizon began to fade a
little.

We had previously decided who would do which jobs in
various types of aircraft, but the Ju 34 was not amongst them.
However, I had usually argued myself into staying in the
cockpit if there was winding to be done, on the grounds of my
broken shoulder. I looked encouragingly at Lorne, who with
much nobility took the handle and got out. We had only
been in the aircraft for perhaps three or four minutes
(although it seemed far longer) and still there had been no
enemy activity, but something else was wrong for Lorne
could not find the hole for the starting handle. He took
refuge in the cockpit, but we could find nothing new there so
he got out again, this time leaving the handle behind so as to
look less conspicuous. Now I felt pretty dejected because if
Lorne with his wide knowledge of aircraft could not find the
hole there did not seem much hope. But a moment later he
did find it, right up on the starboard side of the nose where
you could only reach it by climbing up the port wing and
over the fuselage, or by getting out onto the wing from the
right-hand pilot's seat.

I passed the handle out to him, but just as everything
seemed to be coming right again came the dire words:
"We've had it."

I looked out, and there, walking towards us from the tower,
came the aircraft's rightful crew. Three of them. Three
NCOs of the Luftwaffe.

Evidently we had very nearly had it, but perhaps
something could be salvaged from the wreck, so I turned off
all the cocks and switches and scrambled out of the door just
as the crew arrived. If in doubt salute, especially in
Germany, so I saluted as smartly as this rather scruffy
Gefreiter could manage and the captain said something
which I took to mean "Have you been checking the aircraft?"

so I said: *"Ja."* Then followed an order which I did not
understand at all until it was repeated in the universal sign
language of airfields. Doubtless I looked a very stupid
airman—some dumb Pole, perhaps—but be that as it may I
was being told to to wind the engine for them. Somehow the
boot seemed to have got on to the wrong foot for now they
were stealing the aircraft from us and we were being
expected to help, but I had no choice and I climbed up on
the wing behind them.

I hoped it would start first shot, for clearly our situation
would not stand the strain of fiddling with a recalcitrant
engine. I wound with a will but I was short of puff and the
starter only emitted a feeble whine. At last the pilot engaged
the clutch, but the prop only gave a couple of turns with no
sign of life. I was exhausted, so I waved frantically to Lorne
who was fidgetting about on the ground, and then produced
to the pilot my longest bit of German yet: *"Mein Kamerad
kommt."* This time the engine started and with much relief
we slid off the wing and watched our hopes rumble away
across the field and lift off into the distance. I wonder
whether that crew ever knew of the drama in which they had
unwittingly played a part? It would have been quite a story
to tell in the mess: how their aircraft was started for them by
two RAF flight lieutenants. But on the other hand they could
have been severely disciplined for failing to spot the
imposters.

Now we urgently needed to get out of sight and take stock,
so we retreated towards a rather strange, thatched, barn-like
structure which we had seen a couple of hundred yards from
the main buildings. It looked deserted and we hoped it
would provide cover from which we could watch for another
suitable aircraft. On the way to it we passed the train on
which we had left our belts and thought it might be wise to
put them somewhere safer, but to our horror we found
soldiers in steel helmets and armed to the teeth apparently
searching the wagons. We jumped to the conclusion that
they were searching for us, but a little reflection suggested
that they were probably a guard who were going to travel on
the train. Kupper was a big Luftwaffe supply base and the
train was loaded with all manner of munitions in addition to
our dummy pistols.

Two leather belts with two wooden pistols, where did you
travel? To Russia? To the Balkans? Italy? Were they found

by a soldier in Smolensk who had lost his own and then wore them into Russian captivity? Did they find their way into the Gestapo office in Belgrade, to be used as evidence against innocent Yugoslavs? Maybe the answer was less romantic and they were returned to Sagan as evidence against us.

The barn—if barn it was—proved to be an enigma. It was a wooden building, sunk half below ground level. It had a thatched roof, but the pitch was so nearly flat that it couldn't have been seriously meant to keep out the rain. Inside were two floors, the upper partially boarded and reached from outside by a ramp which could admit a wagon. On the upper door was a notice forbidding wagons over a certain weight to enter, and reaching from the ground to the roof was shuttering for twelve concrete pillars, not yet poured. There was a thermometer with two marks evidently denoting maximum and minimum temperatures, but the purpose of the whole place was inscrutable; so, as there was no sign of recent activity, we concluded that it was a good place from which to watch the airfield, and we took up a position by a small window in the roof. We were fairly inconspicuous, but just in case of trouble I pulled a few boxes round us and settled down to recover from the recent trauma. Then I wished I had taken more care because a few minutes later the upper door creaked open, revealing a soldier. He peered in, but did not see us in the poor light, then went down and opened the bottom door and a party of people came in. We froze and stayed frozen in acute discomfort for the next four hours, during which time we managed to see that the people below appeared to be Russian prisoners of war who were rooting about in the sandy floor for potatoes. Was the place just a potato store? But if so why the concrete pillars?

Evidently the crisis was going to come when the soldier came to close the door, but after what seemed like eternal cramp and suspense it was closed without incident and they all went away. By now it was mid-afternoon and in case there was another visitation we got out of this trap without delay.

Out on the airfield we saw a Focke-Wulf 'Weihe', the standard twin engined trainer of the Luftwaffe. We guessed it would be simple enough and although we saw more than one engine as a handicap, something had to be done. We had not eaten for thirty six hours and doubted whether we would be any use at all by the next day.

Hesitation had lost us our chance with the Junkers and so

we walked boldly out to the 'Weihe', only to find a man working in the cockpit.

Foiled again.

The time had come to make ourselves scarce. We had been wandering around doing rather odd things long enough for one day, and we had the small matter of our belts and pistols on our consciences. So we set off round the perimeter track to return to the safety of our haycocks. However, a fresh hazard soon befell us. Beside the track was a Luftwaffe man cutting grass with a sickle, probably as food for his rabbits. We wondered whether to salute him, but we couldn't identify his rank and we dithered. Germans loved being saluted, but this had proved quite a problem because we not only had to remember to salute in the German style, but we could not always recognise the endless different uniforms and insignia of rank: it could be just as disastrous to be pulled up for not saluting as to salute a private soldier—or worse still, a postman. Just as we passed him I decided that this one probably deserved respect, but I made only a very half hearted gesture, while Lorne did nothing. Then a moment later we were stopped by a roar of rage and the man, who was actually a senior NCO, shouted at Lorne:

"Können sie nicht grüssen?" ("Can't you salute?")

Lorne failed to comprehend and stood looking sheepish and decidedly disorderly. Then the question was repeated and so he tried saying:

"Ja. Entschuldigung." ("Yes. Sorry.")

This, fortunately, was the right answer.

"So. Grüssen sie mich."

I gave the lead; we both saluted briskly, then turned about and retreated hastily to the safety of our haycocks, which we reached still dazed by yet another lucky escape.

During the night we tried to get some food. We thought of burglary, but it seemed too risky. We did get into a vegetable garden, but all we could find was a couple of lettuces, it being too early in the season for anything much more solid. We had another go at baking potatoes, but the results were no better, so in the small hours we went to bed unfed and this time we wore our tunics inside out to avoid the hayseed trouble. We were too exhausted to sleep much or to keep warm and we were very ready to creep out in the morning and try to shave with our ever blunter blades. In eight days we had slept for roughly twenty four hours, walked ninety miles and eaten twenty ounces of food. We felt like it and must have looked like it, but when we got back onto the airfield the adrenalin started to flow once again.

There were no likely looking aircraft in sight so we wandered among the buildings, where we went into a canvas hangar which evidently had once housed gliders. We wished there were still some there to play with (we were pretty far gone!), but all we found was aircraft drop tanks. By this time, although we had walked only about a mile and a half, we were totally exhausted again, adrenalin or no adrenalin. We could not go on wandering about among the buildings where we might well be challenged, so we sat down on the grass, only a couple of hundred yards from the main buildings, but reasonably out of sight. The place was a maintenance unit working on Focke-Wulf 190s, Heinkel 111s and Weihes, none of which were much use to us, so we had to hope for a visitor. Actually, we were past caring whether we were caught or not and even talked about deliberately getting caught if nothing turned up before night time. We were not quite reduced to giving ourselves up, but thought we might look over any aircraft we could find, learning their controls for future reference, and get caught in the process. We toyed with going to the airmen's mess for a meal, but never plucked up courage to try. We destroyed our identity papers and local maps, keeping only the air navigation maps, and we waited disconsolately for a visitor.

After an hour—during which no one questioned our unairmanlike behaviour— a small biplane, a Gotha 145, landed and the pilot left it where the Junkers had been. No use, we thought. It won't have enough fuel unless full, which it can't be because it has just come from somewhere else. Excuses, excuses. However, as it might soon be refuelled, we continued to sit idly by.

Then, suddenly, and not before time, we cursed ourselves for fools. Wasn't there a fair wind for Sweden?—and mightn't there be enough petrol after all? Then just as we started out to have a look the pilot sent someone to fetch his parachute so we had to do another pointless circuit of the buildings and collapse again on the grass.

It seemed there was no likelihood of the aircraft being flown again soon, so after a few minutes we tried again and this time we reached it safely. We knew nothing of the type, but it looked promising, with two open cockpits and a fairly powerful engine. We got in and found that it did have sufficient fuel, but what we could not find was a starting handle. Then we saw a similar aircraft standing in the doorway of a nearby hangar with engine and cockpit covers on. Nothing venture nothing gain, so we walked over, took the covers off, removed the handle, methodically replaced the covers and set off back to our own machine, expecting at any moment to be asked what we were doing. But there were no irate shouts, and with all weariness again forgotten I hopped hopefully into the cockpit. The controls looked straightforward, but I could get no petrol pressure by pulling a toggle marked *'Handpumpe'*. Lorne tried winding, but we got not so much as a kick and it was then, as he came back to investigate, that I saw a *Feldwebel* walking out towards us:

"*Was wollen Sie mit die Maschine?*"

So. Our luck had run out at last. It was the end and I could think of no other answer than:

"*Wir sind Englische Offiziere.*"

Surprisingly, he behaved as though this were an every day occurence: "*Ach so. Komm mit.*"

He took us off to his office where we explained who we were and where we came from. The general attitude was one of interest and amusement until a pompous officer arrived and expressed disgust, especially over our wearing German uniform, which I suppose we had defiled; but no one took much notice of him. We were trying to look like British officers again but we evidently still looked like Luftwaffe because a pilot who was in the office trying to fill up a form turned to me and asked how to do it. A tribute to the makers of our uniforms, but quite an embarrassment to him when he found out who he was talking to.

We were taken to the guard room and locked in separate cells. I was given a cup of *ersatz* coffee which I gulped down and promptly nearly fainted, then I dozed until a *Feldwebel* arrived from the camp with a van and five Tommy gunners. In the guard room, where there was a collection of indignant senior officers, we were told to remove our trousers and boots, but that did not seem to us to befit the dignity of British officers so we protested. It made no difference, so we said we would protest to the Kommandant—but that, they explained, would have to wait, as the Kommandant was back at the camp. Now the scene was quickly reduced to farce as two Flight

Lieutenants of the Royal Air Force, dressed in underpants and Luftwaffe tunics, stood giggling and making facetious remarks while the German officers snorted and the van was backed up to the guard room steps. The Tommy gunners, who fortunately saw the funny side too, stood at the ready as these two desperate criminals, who could not have walked another half mile even for a square meal, climbed in and were driven the few miles back to captivity.

It was eight days since, full of hope, we had walked out through the gates of the camp; and now our flight had been wiped off the departures board and there was not another one due for years. But just then we were passed caring.

Back at the camp we scrambled out of the van and found the Kommandant waiting for us. Colonel von Lindeiner was tall and stately, a soldier of the old school and reputedly sometime Adjutant to the Kaiser. Summoning what dignity I could I wished him good afternoon, but he only snorted in disgust and turned away. Not surprising, perhaps, as dressed only in tunics and underpants we were scarcely a credit to the Luftwaffe. We had already caused him a great deal of trouble and we were going to cause him more.

The cooler was still full with the rest of the Delousing Party, who had been caught so promptly and were serving the regulation fourteen days solitary, so we were put in cells in the guard room, where I went straight to sleep until a guard arrived with food and clothes from my room in the camp. This considerate service seemed almost too good to be true, but that didn't stop me from tucking in to biscuits, butter and spam—not that I could eat very much after a long period of near starvation.

That evening, who should blow in to see me but *Hauptmann* Pieber.

"Ah, Mr Mawrison," he drawled. "I was so sorry to hear what happened to you. It was most unfortunate, such a fine effort. Really, I am most sorry about it."

Pieber understood the handling of prisoners. Even when tempers were at their hottest he never lost his own, but always had a joke ready, often against himself, which pacified an angry crowd when military discipline might have provoked real trouble. He was a Viennese, and depending partly on this he maintained a friendly attitude towards the Kriegies— often, no doubt, with an ulterior motive, but on this occasion

I thought he was sincere and I thanked him politely. After all, it had been a fine effort, although alas! not fine enough, for nothing fails quite so completely as failure.

The next day brought a visitor whose interest was definitely on the side of the Reich. *Stabs Feldwebel* Kracht, he who had brought us back from Kupper, had a long conversation which kept leading back to how we had got out and what we had done. Of course, he did not want to know anything which I might regard as a military secret, or which involved my friends, but it was apparent, so he said, that we could not have got the equipment needed to pass the gate without the help of German soldiers: "—and traitorship of that sort, Mr Morison, must be as repugnant to you as it is us."

Well, yes. I quite agreed, but pointed out that if it was to my advantage I was prepared to condone it.

He turned to the subject of aircraft, in which he could see that there must be a fascination. Had he been a younger man he would have chosen to fly in this war himself, and he could see how we would wish to fly home, but wouldn't it have been terribly dangerous? The aircraft, only a light trainer, was not intended for long flights; it had insufficient petrol and its instruments were unserviceable. Certainly, in any case, we would have been shot down. Again I agreed with him, so far as the fascination of flying was concerned and particularly the fascination of bombing German cities, but that did not seem to be quite what he wanted and finally he went away. I hoped none the wiser.

There were several Germans besides us in the guardroom cells, but they were taking their punishment pretty easily, and one day when I called the guard to ask for a newspaper I saw them all sitting in the passage chatting with him. The guard refused the paper, but a little later there was a noise of "Pst! Pst!" from the corner of my cell and a paper was pushed through a hole in the wall, after which I got a regular delivery of the *Volkischer Beobachter*. The news when we left the camp had been that the last of the German army in North Africa had capitulated, and now the first news which I got from the outer world was that our troops had landed on Pantellaria, so things were looking up.

Soon there was a formal interrogation by an *Oberleutnant* Roske, a runt-like little man. I declared the usual formula, refusing to tell him anything, but he was insistent that I should make a statement as to where I had been, because, as he rightly pointed out, my circumstances were somewhat compromising. Naturally he assured me that it was solely for my own safety, but no doubt it was also for his because the more he could keep me out of trouble the less would he have to explain to his superiors why his prisoners were wandering about Germany trying to steal Luftwaffe property. Finally I made a statement to the effect that I had escaped from Stalag Luft III on 10 June, and that after spending some time in the vicinity searching for an airfield I was recaptured at Kupper on 18 June. This had the merit of being no more than he knew already and of being true—and moreover it seemed to satisfy him.

The next official function was the taking of photographs. Lorne and I were obliged to dress up in our Luftwaffe uniforms and pose for the camera. It seemed simple enough, but Pieber, who was among the onlookers, was not satisfied:

"Come along now chentlemen, why are you looking so miserable? Look a little cheerful, please."

"We should look miserable," said Lorne; "we're supposed to be Germans, aren't we?"

This was Pieber's style, and I am sure that if instead of photography he had been supervising a firing party, he would have been the same.

When we had been in the cells for a few days we were put through an odd performance. We were taken separately and unknown to one another to offices in the *Kommandantur* and kept waiting for over an hour. Roske was there and asked me some pointless questions. Then my German uniform was produced and I was told to put it on. Still nothing happened for a long time, but evidently we were waiting for something, and I discovered that a General was visiting the camp and wished to speak to me.

At last the General and his retinue approached and I was led out, but he paid no attention and I was taken straight back to the cells without achieving any apparent object. Lorne was brought out a few moments later and met the General as he entered the hut. He was peered at and asked a few questions, but the whole business remained a mystery, unless they were trying to impress on the General how easy it was to mistake us for the real thing.

After a week the cooler was emptied by the return to the camp of the main Delousing Party, so we moved over from the guard room, and it was then that it began to dawn on us that there was trouble brewing for those who had been caught wearing German uniform which, apart from Lorne and I, included Bob Vanderstok, 'Woody' Wood and 'Ginger' Garwell. Bob, dressed as an *Unteroffizier*, had been in charge of the ill-fated Senior Officers' party which had failed to follow us out through the gate, while Woody and Ginger had also aimed to take an aircraft, but did not get far and anyway were only carrying Luftwaffe caps and belts, which did not seem such a sin.[1]

One day we were all taken to see Roske, whom we found sitting at his desk looking as pompous as possible. He told us that if we cared to give our parole not to escape we could go back to the camp while our case was investigated, but of course we at once declared that as British officers it was our duty to escape and therefore we could give no such parole. Ah! but the investigations, he pointed out, might last half a year, or longer, and the alternative was to remain under arrest. However, we knew very well that once they had extracted our parole the 'investigations' would last for the rest of the war, so there could be only one answer.

Finally I got a bit cross:

"What, anyway, is all this talk about investigating our case? What case? How does it differ from any ordinary case?"

The *Oberleutnant* drew from his desk some of our maps and, pointing to the airfields marked on them, uttered with great solemnity the word: "Espionage."

Then he produced our jemmy and, holding it up, pronounced the equally dreaded word: "Sabotage."

(Somehow these words sounded worse with a German pronunciation).

He then renewed the offer of parole, but as that was a nonrunner he proceeded to play his ace, and assuming as best he could the style of the Gestapo he slowly drew a letter from his desk, solemnly examined it, then held it out to Woody:

"This is to you *Herr* Wood."

"So I see."

Roske opened it and took out a photograph. "So you are married, *Herr* Wood."

[1] In March 1944 Vanderstok escaped through tunnel Harry and eventually reached England.

"Yes."

"And this is your wife and child?"

"Yes."

"Look well at them.   You wish to see them again, no doubt?"

"Like hell I do."

Wood was an Australian; his replies were typically laconic and somehow all this talk of espionage and sabotage began to seem absurd.   Roske's intended sinister drama quickly deteriorated into farce and he had no choice but to return us to the cooler.

The five of us—together with an American who was there because a searching Gestapo officer had found his bed decorated with a drawing of the Führer with a noose round his neck—now became long term residents. I was moved in with Ginger, while Lorne was with Woody, but Bob was always kept on his own. Ginger Garwell had been the pilot of a Lancaster when on 17 April of the previous year his squadron attacked the MAN works at Augsburg, where diesel engines for U-boats were built. The raid was an experiment in using the new four engined bombers in low level precision attacks in daylight and involved flying for 500 miles over enemy territory at a few hundred feet (not to mention 500 miles back if you were still alive, which wasn't very likely as more than half the aircraft were lost). Not surprisingly the casualties were too heavy for the experiment to be repeated and thereafter the RAF heavy bombers seldom operated other than at night. The leader was awarded the VC and meanwhile Ginger languished in Sagan. Fortunately he didn't know at the time that although the panache of the raid captured the imagination of the British public the Ministry of Economic Warfare was not amused, regarding the target as of too low priority to justify such a squandering of scarce resources, and an acrimonious correspondence ensued between the Ministry, the Prime Minister, the Air Ministry and Bomber Command.

Life in the cooler was a strange interlude, but it was not all bad. It transpired that we were now in 'protective custody', rather than under arrest, "because of course, gentlemen, it would be extremely dangerous for you were you to attempt to escape while the enquiry is in progress"—which was probably true. As a result we were allowed Red Cross parcels, books, mail, newspapers and tobacco, and as we got full parcels we did better than those in the camp, where the Kommandant had taken the outrageous step of ordering half parcels because excess food was encouraging too much escaping!

The guards were a mixed lot. There were decent and honest men, shifty and mean men, there were Nazis and there were just ordinary Germans. In charge was *Unteroffizier* Mawr, who was a Nazi and liked to lecture us on the virtues of National Socialism. He claimed to have taken part in the invasion of Norway and one day extolled the glorious feats of the Wehrmacht to the Kriegie in the cell next to mine. He thought he was talking to an Englishman, but unfortunately for him it was a Norwegian who knew very well that a lot of the story was palpable nonsense. A more sympathetic character was a grubby old Austrian peasant of limited vocabulary and a jaundiced view of the war. If you greeted him with the usual: *"Morgen. Was ist heute neues?"*—"What's the news?" the reply would probably be: *"Mensch, alles Scheisse. In Sicilien ist es Scheisse und in Russland ist es grosse Scheisse."* ("Man, everything's shit. In Sicily it's shit and in Russia it's great shit.")

One day he analysed the whole human predicament in a few nicely chosen words: *"Ich bin Soldat, nicht wahr? Und für mich ist alles Scheisse. Sie. Sie sind Offizier und für Sie auch ist alles Scheisse. So. Was haben wir? Mensch, der Krieg ist für jedermann Scheisse."* ("I'm a soldier. Right? And for me everything is shit. You. You're an officer and for you too it's all shit. So. What have we? Man. The war is shit for everyone.")

A simple man, but wise. He was known affectionately to all of us as *'Grosse Scheisse'*.

Most unpleasant of the guards was a very young, very Nazi little horror, the sort who would have done well at Auschwitz; but at Sagan all he could do was to make himself a tiresome nuisance. One day I was extremely rude to him, in English, but he evidently picked out the salient word of abuse. He must have heard it often enough before, but this time he was determined to learn the meaning and he went to consult Lorne:

"What means in English 'Folk'?"

"Ah!" said Lorne, in all innocence. " 'Folk.' Of course—it means people. Like *'Volk'* in German."

"Nein, nein. Not people, 'Folk'."

In the end they never did unravel the problem and perhaps it was just as well for me.

The guards would often get bored and would come into the cells for a chat. One came in and half-shouted that he had good news for us:

"Your troops have landed in Sicily. Yes, you are glad, but I, *Gefreiter* Meyer, I am glad too. Yes. Now we shall see. All this time we have been waiting, and for a soldier to wait is bad. You have been talking about what you will do, but the German army is strong. You will be thrown back—back into the sea!"

This tirade was in German, to which I could not reply as fluently, so I contented myself with: "*Mann wird sehen.* —We shall see."

Discipline in the cooler was fairly slack. We were forbidden to meet or talk to other prisoners, but somehow this did not apply during the weekly visit to the showers, to which we all went together, and anyway we could converse through the windows, leave notes in the lavatory or pop them through the peep holes in cell doors as we went past. One piece of news which passed in this way was that everyone on the Delousing Party had been recaptured except Johnny Stower—whom we had last seen on the road to Halbau—and the Germans were putting it about that an unidentified prisoner, thought to be Johnny, had been shot while resisting arrest. Actually he was in a safe house in Prague, but was later recaptured on the Swiss frontier. When a year later he was in fact shot the excuse once again was 'while resisting arrest'.

One day I was told to get ready for an interview with some high German officers. I had not got my RAF uniform in the cooler, but Ginger had and so, wanting to appear properly dressed, I borrowed his and sallied forth, feeling rather bogus because it bore the ribbons of the DFC and DFM. I had been told that a high officer from the Air Ministry in Berlin wished to speak to me, but most of the nine German officers in the room into which I was led were from the camp and the most senior present was a Lieutenant Colonel who, from the tenor of his questions, appeared to come from Kupper and to want only to collect evidence with which to dispense blame for the lapses in his security. I was told that I had committed very serious offences, that I was to be court martialled and that I might be sentenced to death. Then I was asked a lot of

questions, leading finally to whether we had tried to take a
Junkers 34. The interrogation followed the classic technique
of asking a series of innocuous questions to which it seems
safe to reply, followed by an important one, the refusal to
answer which is an admission of guilt. The wise man says
nothing at all. I should have known better, but this time I
was among the foolish:

"Do you know the aircraft type Ju 34?"

"Yes."

"Ah! How do you know it?"

Umm...a bit awkward that, but ah...: "It's my job to know
it. I'm an Air Force officer."

"When you were on the airfield at Kupper did you see any
of these aircraft?"

Well there were several there so no harm in saying so:
"Yes, there were a number parked by the hangars."

"Did you try to steal one of these aircraft?"

*Oh dear. No good saying 'No' because they almost cer-
tainly know that I did and would be able to tie me in knots
once they knew I was lying.*

"That is a question I am not prepared to answer."

But in effect my reply meant: 'Yes I did.'

They continued to press the point, and having got myself
deeply into a hole I decided that as we had not really done
anything very naughty the best defence before a court would
be the truth, so finally I admitted that we had tried to take
such an aircraft. However, it was a clear case of lack of moral
fibre and failure to follow the simple and safe course of saying
absolutely nothing, which, when the same gang confronted
Lorne was exactly what he did.

At the end I asked on what charges we were to appear
before a court martial. The interpreting officer looked per-
plexed and hastily passed the buck to the man next to him,
who in turn passed it on and so it went round until it could
go no further. Then, hesitatingly and in German, which I
was not supposed to understand, it was admitted that there
was no question of a court martial. The interpreter managed
to make it a slightly less frank admission, but nevertheless
this was a relief. It is not a lot of fun being threatened with
death, even if it seems unlikely, but the Germans were
evidently getting very worked up and were probably being
told from on high that this sort of thing had got to stop and
that they must make an example of us.

One person, anyway, was taking the matter seriously and that was 'Wings' Day, then acting Senior British Officer while Group Captain Massey was in hospital. He wrote to the Protecting Power (Switzerland) requesting an investigation of our case and a copy of his letter reached us in the cooler. His description of the mentality capable of describing our jemmy as an instrument of sabotage was a tonic in itself and the knowledge that the SBO was doing something about our plight was a comfort at the time and in retrospect may well have saved our lives. (Unhappily, no copy of this splendid letter can now be traced).

The Russian Air Force prisoners, whom we used to see working on the construction of our compound, lived in huts opposite our window and we could see them through chinks in the screen. In the evenings they sang plaintive and monotonous songs to the twanging of home made stringed instruments which, alas, did not quite live up to our romantic image of the balalaika. One of these Russians was employed in sweeping out the cells in the cooler, and it was just another of the absurdities of war that he, a Russian Captain, was cleaning up for me, an English Flight Lieutenant. Naturally we called him 'Ivan', and we had some wonderful conversations in a mixture of German, English, French and mime. One of his masterpieces was a comparison of the American Tomahawk fighter with the Spitfire, both of which he had flown against the Luftwaffe in Russia. To the accompaniment of much gesticulation it went something like this:

"Tomahawk: *Vitesse gut. Virage nicht gut.* [Speed good. Turn poor]."

"Spitfire: *Virage prima. Steig gut.* [Turn prima. Climb good]."

"Tomahawk: *Sechs Maschinen Gewehr. Nicht gut.* [Six machine guns. No good.]"

"Spitfire: *Zwei Kanonen.* [Two cannons.]"

Then, as his thumb closed on an imaginary firing button, he gave a raucous imitation of cannon, fire and an ecstatic grin spread across his face in which you could see Messerschmits and Heinkels dissolving under a hail of shells from the Spit. One expressive word followed:

"PRIMA!"

Sometimes, however, communication broke down. Seeing a pile of cabbages outside the window, and feeling the need of some fresh vegetables, we had a quick word with Ivan through the peep hole in the door and uttered the word *"Kohl"* (cabbage), as well as describing round shapes in the air with our hands. Ivan repeated *"Kohl"*, beamed and disappeared. When he returned he managed to convey that the loot was safely stowed in the stove in the passage, but alas that was only too appropriate and we found that Ivan had filled the stove with coal.

After we had sweltered in the mid-summer heat for several weeks Jerry Hill and Jan Staubo arrived in the cooler. Jerry was a fluent German speaker and ace contact man with intimate associations among the guards, but it would not have been etiquette to ask whether it was this or just plain courage which had enabled them to climb the wire without challenge (they needed the courage anyway). Alas, one of them then fell and twisted his ankle, following which they walked straight into an off duty soldier who chanced to be strolling through the woods just outside the wire and that was the end of their exploit.

Soon after this we were joined by Major Jerry M Sage, a large and muscular American parachutist who, on the way to hospital, had torn open the doors of the ambulance and started walking impromptu to Czechoslovakia. Jerry Hill, Jan and the Major were a sociable trio as well as hotly *'Deutschfeindlch'* ('anti-German' is a weak translation), and one evening they organised a little community singing. The guard took this as a breach of the peace and ordered them to stop, but they declared that there was no rule against singing and the noise continued. Then the guard, fearing rebellion, phoned for assistance, but nothing much happened until in the middle of the night, when at last everyone was sleeping quietly, it appeared that a madman had entered the cooler and let loose a tornado. It was none other than the Kommandant, who burst into the Major's cell shouting:

"Major Sage! *MAJOR SAGE!*"

The Major, who was not only very large, but also very loose limbed, rubbed his eyes and started to uncoil himself slowly on the top of his bunk until suddenly the Kommandant drew his gun, whereupon the Major, who understood the meaning of guns, sat up promptly on the edge of his bed where he was subjected to a torrent of abuse, accompanied by much waving of the gun. This was not the Kommandant we knew. Normally he was dignified and courteous, but stories of similar outbursts kept coming in to the cooler and it seemed that he must be losing his grip. There was even a rumour that he had told the Swiss Commission that he could not sleep at night for nightmares about escaping prisoners (perhaps he was counting them instead of sheep), but anyway escaping was evidently driving him to distraction. It was not surprising for there was not a lot that he could do about it. A thousand intelligent and active young men, all anxious to go home and with plenty of time to find a way, were bound to be more than a match for anything the Kommandant could pit against them, at least so long as the rules treated escaping as a sport.

Whenever more than a few Kriegies got out the Gestapo would come in to search the camp, which was a serious loss of face for the Luftwaffe, and no doubt severe reprimands came from the High Command. He must also have been worried that he would be ordered to carry out reprisals and it was said, after one mass escape, that he told the SBO that if he were ordered to shoot prisoners he would shoot himself first— and that one could believe for he was an honourable man. The regular Wehrmacht and Luftwaffe hated the political police and when the Gestapo came in would never give them any help. The ferrets, who knew a thing or two about the ways of Kriegies, justifiably regarded the Gestapo as bungling amateurs as well as intruders on their patch. Anyone who was not a professional Kriegie guard interfered at his peril and the classic case was when a Wehrmacht General came to inspect the camp. He came in a car, which he left inside the compound while he went on his rounds, and that was the first mistake. The car was in charge of a chauffeur, but it was not long before the simple soul accepted an offer of refreshment from a kindly Kriegie. That was the second mistake, but the ultimate folly was to leave the car unlocked. By the time the General left the compound his car had been stripped of its contents, which included some highly confidential documents relating to the treatment of prisoners of war. All unwitting, he had been favourably impressed by the well mannered behaviour in Stalag Luft III and no doubt congratulated the Kommandant. Next day, however, the hapless von Lindeiner was obliged to send for the SBO and appeal to him for the missing documents to be returned forthwith, failing which he feared that there would be really serious trouble, and no doubt for him as well as for the Kriegies.

Returned they were, but the Kriegies had the last laugh for they had affixed the German censor's stamp *'Geprüft'* and had added: 'Approved by HM officers, Stalag Luft III'. Small wonder that poor von Lindeiner was losing his nerve.

When we had been in the cooler for six weeks all the wearers of German uniform were gathered together and we were told that the High Command had found our case to be one for Kommandant's disciplinary action only and that he had sentenced us to ten days arrest. We pointed out that we had already done forty days and so would presumably be returning to the camp forthwith, but we were reminded that we had only been in protective custody, whereas now we were under strict arrest; and not only would we have to serve another ten days, but worse still would have no more Red Cross parcels. Now that there was nothing left to speculate about life became tedious. The heat was stifling, there was little to eat, books and crosswords and conversation seemed boring, and although there were really only a few days to wait I became sceptical of ever seeing the compound again and, as it turned out, I was right. Less than half way through the ten days the door opened and in came *Unteroffizier* Mawr, who peremptorily ordered me to take my things and go into cell number eight. A moment later I heard the same order given to Lorne and the sound was ominous indeed. Birds of a feather flock together and in cell number eight was Jerry Hill. Jan Staubo, with whom he had climbed the wire, had already been released, and we were now in the same class as Jerry, who was regarded by the Germans—and from their point of view entirely justifiably—as a very bad character and a likely candidate for Colditz.

The British saw it otherwise and after the war he was awarded the *MBE* 'for services in prison camps'.

Little was known of Colditz. Only five people had been sent there from Sagan and none had returned. It was thought of as the *'Straflager'* (punishment camp), but what that meant no one knew; and although the word had grim overtones I had never given the matter much thought. To consider the possibility of being sent to Colditz would have been to put oneself in the same class as 'Czecho' Chaloupka, or 'Bush' Parker, or Jack Best, or Bill Goldfinch, or Peter Van

Rood—and that would have been presumptuous for they were the aces of the escaping business. Now, however, Colditz became the subject of intense speculation, to which was added a rumour—picked up by Jerry—that the Luftwaffe was building a new *Straflager*, and if that were so we hoped that we would be sent there instead, because Colditz was an army camp and anyway it would be an advantage to be a founder member of a new camp.

We must have been nervous about our future because we incessantly made feeble jokes about dungeons and whipping posts. The best joke of all, at least we thought so at the time, involved a scene in which the Kommandant arrived at the last moment and said: 'Gentlemen, this has all been a ghastly mistake.' 'Ghastly mistake' became the catch phrase of the moment and was enough to send us into fits of laughter. The nervousness, together with the new sense of uncertain adventure, made this a hilarious period, so hilarious indeed that one evening I bounced so much on my bed that it collapsed onto the bed below. Happily, no one was injured and it was simply the signal for more hysterical laughter. In its way this was a happy time, but it ended one day when I came in from the afternoon's half hour of walking round our little sandy exercise patch, to be greeted by Jerry with the words:

"Well my boy, you've had it. *Straflager* for you."

The three of us were to be ready to leave at three o'clock the next morning, by train. All our stuff was sent down from our rooms and the quantity which we had managed to accumulate over a year was amazing. There were kit bags, suit cases, even a packing case and the unfortunate Mawr had to search everything before it was packed, muttering as he did so about capitalists and wealthy fathers. There was more than we could carry and half had to be sent after us by freight train.

The path to the station led through the woods, the same ones into which the Delousing Party had vanished, and as it would be dark it looked as though there might be a chance to run for it. We made some preparations, but for my part I hoped that there would be no running because I did not like being shot at, and anyway the chances of success were remote if you weren't equipped with all the necessary papers, money, maps and so on. When the time came we were collected by a bad tempered *Unteroffizier*, with a Tommy gunner and an interpreter. For three prisoners deemed so desperate that they must be sent to Colditz it seemed a poor, even an insulting escort, particularly since we had rated five Tommy gunners on the journey back from Kupper. Nevertheless, as we made our way through the dark woods it proved enough to discourage any running and in due course we boarded the train.

Travel on the German railways was a slow business. As in England military traffic had priority and even the slogans had the same flavour. In England it was: 'Make way for the guns on the lines behind the lines', while now we saw everywhere huge posters proclaiming: *'Die Räder müssen rollen fur den Sieg.'* ('The wheels must roll for victory.') By lunch time we had covered the hundred and thirty miles to Leipzig, but there we had to wait two hours for a connection. Jerry had had the guards in the camp eating out of his hand, but unfortunately this one was new and had probably been warned of the risk of being corrupted by this fluent and smooth-talking Englander. He was clearly going to need a lot of training in how to treat Kriegies, and at this moment he thought that the right course was to put us in the station lock up while we waited for the connection. They were the most noisome, dark, disgusting little boxes imaginable and we refused to go in, demanding to see an officer. When one arrived Jerry exploded like an insulted thunder cloud, saying that we were British Officers, not criminals, and that it was a disgrace to suggest putting us in a place like that. To a German officer we were probably nearer to being brother officers than enemies and he spluttered his apologies, but regretted that he could think of nothing better so we solved the problem for him by declaring that we would sit on the platform and wait there, to which he agreed.

We sat tucking in to quantities of Canadian butter and other goodies, as much to impress the passers by with the folly of 'preferring guns to butter' as to nourish ourselves against whatever might be in store. The Tommy gunner watched us closely, but at one point he went away, leaving his gun in the hands of the interpreter, who held it on his knee at arm's length as though terrified that it might go off. This would have been the moment to run for it, except that we could think of no satisfactory answer to the question: 'What do you do when you find yourself in the middle of Leipzig, in RAF uniform, on a summer afternoon, with no money, no papers and no food?'

The final twenty five miles to Colditz took another three hours and as the train puffed into the station we saw what must surely be the castle standing high above the little country town which nestled on the banks of the River Mulde. It looked grim indeed and we made few jokes as we sweated up the hill with our baggage. One, two, three great wooden gates closed behind us, each one of which seemed to say: 'Abandon hope all ye who enter in', although even that would have been better than *'Arbeit macht frei'* ('Work sets you free'), that terrible sick joke which stood above the gates of Auschwitz. Then the fourth gate closed behind us and we were free within the narrow confines of Oflag IVC, the so called *Straflager*, once even described in the British press as 'The Nazi Hell Camp'—although happily the truth was to prove somewhat different.

'WANTED MEN'

Special edition of the German 'Criminal Police Gazette' issued by the State Criminal Police Office in Berlin on 16 June, 1943, six days after the 'Delousing Party' escape from Stalag Luft III. The main part reads: "Escape of British and American Air Force officers from the Luftwaffe camp No.3 at Sagan. Of the 26 escaped Air Force officers the following are still at large: Lt William Hill, F/Lt Walter Morison, F/O John Stower, F/O Patrick [Lorne] Welch. Further energetic search. Capture them. Morison, Stower and Welch are pictured below." *(IWM HU21187.)*

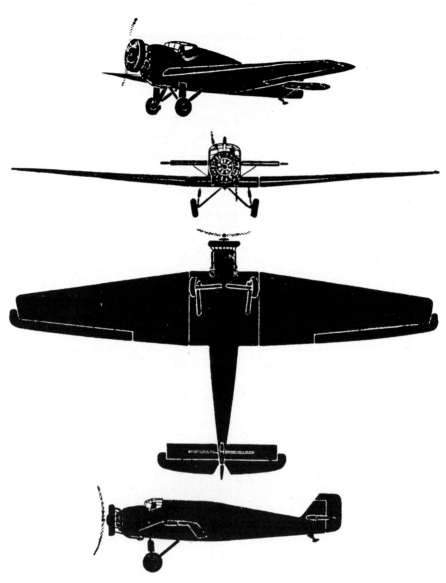

JUNKERS W34 (Obsolescent)

Trainer

Span 60′–5″   Length 33′–7″   Height 11′–5″

'The one that got away.' A Junkers W34.
Silhouettes from contemporary spotters' handbook.

'The one we didn't get away with.' A Gotha 145.

'Obergefreiter' Welch and 'Gefreiter' Morison.
Above: Back in the camp and looking the worse for wear. *(IWM HU21188.)*
Below: At a later photo-call and looking a bit brighter. *(IWM HU21189.)*

To all Prisoners of War!

The escape from prison camps is no longer a sport!

Germany has always kept to the Hague Convention and only punished recaptured prisoners of war with minor disciplinary punishment.

Germany will still maintain these principles of international law.

But England has besides fighting at the front in an honest manner instituted an illegal warfare in non combat zones in the form of gangster commandos, terror bandits and sabotage troops even up to the frontiers of Germany.

They say in a captured secret and confidential English military pamphlet,

THE HANDBOOK
OF MODERN IRREGULAR
WARFARE:

". . . the days when we could practise the rules of sportsmanship are over. For the time being, every soldier must be a potential gangster and must be prepared to adopt their methods whenever necessary."

"The sphere of operations should always include the enemy's own country, any occupied territory, and in certain circumstances, such neutral countries as he is using as a source of supply."

England has with these instructions opened up a non military form of gangster war!

Germany is determined to safeguard her homeland, and especially her war industry and provisional centres for the fighting fronts. Therefore it has become necessary to create strictly forbidden zones, called death zones, in which all unauthorised trespassers will be immediately shot on sight.

Escaping prisoners of war, entering such death zones, will certainly lose their lives. They are therefore in constant danger of being mistaken for enemy agents or sabotage groups.

Urgent warning is given against making future escapes!

In plain English: Stay in the camp where you will be safe! Breaking out of it is now a damned dangerous act.

The chances of preserving your life are almost nil!

All police and military guards have been given the most strict orders to shoot on sight all suspected persons.

Escaping from prison camps has ceased to be a sport!

The ominous warning from the *Oberkommando der Wehrmacht*. Its final words, 'Escaping from prison camps has ceased to be a sport', were all too true.

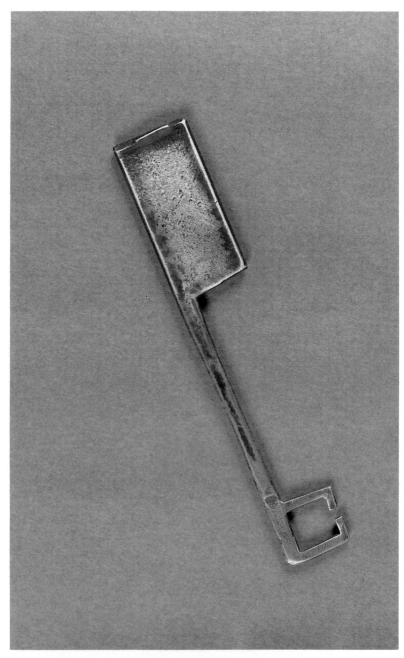

Skeleton key for the old-fashioned locks in Colditz castle.
(Actual length 14.5 cms.)

The Colditz Glider.

Above: Quarter-scale model built by Martin Francis to prove that the design was airworthy. It does not show the detailed finish of the original——but it flies perfectly. *(Martin Francis.)*

Below: Martin Francis *(centre)* with the model, flanked by Jack Best *(left)* and Bill Goldfinch. *(Martin Francis.)*

Above: George Drew's chess set with, in foreground, the tools made by the author and with which George did his whittling. The chess pieces, from left, represent a walrus, *kohlrabi* (a vegetable much hated by POWs), 'February', (George always carved a figure for the month during which he was working), George Drew, unidentified, Hecate. *(George Drew.)*

Below: Box lid for chess set with representations of Colditz POWs. From left: Colonel Tod, Mike Edwards, Mike Willet, Hamish Hamilton, 'Bush' Parker, George Drew, Mike Farr, Pat Farr and John Beaumont. Centre is a still producing 'Jam Alc' and far right is Mephistopheles. *(George Drew.)*

CHAPTER NINE

Colditz—Oflag IVC

LIVING in a castle is...well it's different! Mind you, there were a number of people at Colditz for whom living in a castle was an everyday affair. These were the 'Prominente'— or some of them anyway—and then there was a rather socially okay group for whom life in castles would not have been wholly unfamiliar, and they were dubbed 'The Bullingdon' after the Oxford society for to people. The Prominente (pronounced *Prominenty*) were really hostages, although the Germans would never have admitted it. They were a small group of POWs who were related to eminent persons and included Viscount Lascelles (the King), Giles Romilly (Churchill), Michael Alexander (whom the Germans believed, wrongly, to be the nephew of Field Marshal Alexander), and a couple of earls, Haig and Hopetoun. But you definitely had to be well connected, politically or militarily, and thus Lord Arundell of Wardour,the 14th and last baron, escaped being a Prominenter. They were kept under strict supervision, being locked in specially guarded quarters at night, and they suffered other restrictions, but they also had privileges such as being taken for walks in the country. As a bargaining counter they would scarcely have weighed heavily in the scales against the fate of Hitler, but theirs wasn't a very comfortable situation and as the war approached its end the Germans did indeed make a rather feeble effort to exploit them.

Quite apart from these special cases the community at Colditz was unique. When Jerry, Lorne and I arrived there were three hundred or so inmates, mostly soldiers, quite a number of airmen and a few sailors. The basic qualification for being there was either that you were a persistent escaper, or that you were *'Deutschfeindlich'*, but there were others ranging from behind-the-lines operators with a glib enough tongue, or the good luck, to talk themselves out of the hands of the Gestapo, to people whose only offence was to have been a Sapper in a camp where a tunnel was discovered; after all, it's engineers who dig tunnels, so why not get rid of all the engineer officers to Colditz? One of the inmates had become

Colditz.

A local postcard sent home attached to a standard POW letter form. It shows the courtyard at Colditz, probably before the war.

a Kriegie through absolutely no fault of his own, and this was Tommy Catlow. Tommy was a submarine commander and was at Gibraltar in the spare submarine crew when a call came from Malta that he was urgently needed there to take over a boat. There was a squadron of Wellingtons in Gib on its way to the Middle East, via Malta, so he went with them, but things went ill. First one engine failed, then, in sight of the island, they were warned that an air raid was in progress and they should stand off to the north until it cleared. Inevitably, they were slowly losing height, so this was bad news; and it was even worse that they were to go north, for Sicily was less than fifty miles away, and it was no time before a couple of Messerschmitts appeared and shot them down. They were carrying stores for Malta, stacked all over the aircraft, and when they crash landed on Sicily Tommy ended up smothered in baked beans.

Also now in Colditz, and not quite understanding why they deserved this distinction, were this couple of innocent customers who had just wanted to borrow an aircraft from the Luftwaffe; only borrow it. The Goons could gladly have had it back if they cared to collect it from Sweden.

If anyone were to set out deliberately to assemble such a diverse and fascinating group of people they wouldn't succeed in a hundred years. They were individualists almost by definition, and as we all had the Kriegie's natural instinct not to ask questions about what did not concern us it was difficult to make more than superficial contact. This was particularly so with those who had family or colleagues still at large in German occupied territories whom they might compromise by a careless word.

The Germans had written themselves a recipe for trouble when they conceived the idea of gathering persistent escapers into a specially secure prison. Persistent escapers were by definition expert escapers and a castle was not a clever choice. Castles are designed to keep the enemy out, not to keep him in, and the result was a hot-bed of escaping, with more escapes per hundred Kriegies and more who actually got home than from any other camp. Nevertheless, the will to escape was no more intense than at Sagan—indeed it was arguably less so—but the scene was certainly different, and not only because of the technical problems posed by a castle compared with those in a hutted camp. There was an effective central organisation, but, to this ex-Sagan Kriegie anyway, it didn't seem to have quite the edge that there was under Roger Bushell. At Colditz the attitude to the Goons was poles apart from that at Sagan, where it was not only considered discourteous to be rude to Goons, but also counter-productive. Goon baiting could waste good escaping time while you stood on *Appel*, or might call down restrictions of one sort or another on your head, but at Colditz it was all the rage and could easily lead to a scene like when we were all standing in the courtyard on *Appel*:

Enter the Goon second in command, the fat and pompous Major Amthor, wearing a flowing cape and preceded by an NCO.

NCO: *"Achtung für den Herr Major, Stellvertreter des Kommandantens."* ("Attention for the Major, second in command to the Kommandant").

Kriegies: "Baa-aa Baa-aa. Baa-aa."

Repeat several times.

Fat, pompous, and now furious Major orders the courtyard to be cleared. Sentries herd bleating Kriegies indoors. Kriegies reappear at upper windows. Bleating continues. Paper bags full of water rain down. FP&F Major orders the Kriegies to be cleared from the windows.

NCO: *"Zurück vom Fenster oder wird erschossen!*—Back from the windows or we fire!"

Kriegies: "Baa-aa. Baa-aa. Baa-aa."

Sentries take aim.

NCO: *"Feuer!"*

Kriegies duck. The walls are five feet thick. No-one is hurt.

An event like this happened one day when an inspector from the Protecting Power (Switzerland) was visiting the camp, scaring him stiff and probably leading to the British press references to the 'Nazi Hell Camp'.

There had been a castle at Colditz for nearly a thousand years. At one time it was the seat of the kings of Saxony, but more recently it had been a prison, a mental hospital and, after the arrival of Hitler, an offshoot of the Buchenwald concentration camp, then a training centre for the Hitler Youth. This was a pretty gruesome history and by rights the place should have been teeming with ghosts, but there didn't seem to be any. In 1939 it became a *Sonderlager* (a special camp) for POWs, but never a *Straflager*. The first inmates were Belgian, Dutch, French and Polish officers who were serving in the forces of their own countries, soon to be followed by the British. Each nationality was housed in its own quarters and there was international rivalry, not least as to who could be most anti-Goon. After a while the Goons realised their mistake in mixing this explosive cocktail and moved out the continentals, but the tradition of Goon baiting survived to the end of the war.

A good, solid castle was on the whole a more comfortable place to live than in wooden huts, despite the confined space. Most of the rooms were bigger than at Sagan; mine had fourteen in it, including Lorne, but it had just been redecorated after the French, the last of the continentals, had been moved out. It had a superb, although tantalising, view over the town and surrounding countryside, and as prisons go was very pleasant. We had separate dining rooms, where there were cooking stoves and where we arranged ourselves in 'messes' of about eight people. We had full parcels at this time, and a few days after my arrival I wrote home to say that we had just invited friends from another mess to a dinner party, where the menu included mixed grill, meat pie, jam tart, sardines on toast, coffee and raisin wine.

There was a cook-house from which the Goon rations were produced, mostly soup, potatoes, bread and margarine. The soup usually consisted largely of swedes or the dreaded *Kohlrabi*, also known to the French as *'rutabagas'*. Delicate young *Kohlrabi* may be all very well, but allowed by the Goons to grow into huge solid lumps of wood they were less than digestible. The Goon menu for the day would be chalked on a blackboard outside the cook-house and showed a distinct lack of variety. A disconsolate Frenchman gazing at it one day was heard to bemoan: *"Ah, les rutas, toujours les rutas."*—and that about summed it up. The soup, or whatever, was issued in huge aluminium buckets known as *Kübels*, which could also be used to collect hot water from the kitchen boilers, so that you could have a bath, for there were bathrooms with real baths, but only running cold water. Captain Pemberton How, who was impolitely known as 'Pembum' and who was an innkeeper in real life, enjoyed his comforts and was a great devotee of the hot bath. It was a pleasure to see his portly form wallowing in the steam and it was an even greater pleasure to get in after him.

The courtyard may have been small, paved with stone cobbles and surrounded by stone walls, but that did not stop people playing violent games in it, of which a favourite was stoolball, something like rugger, where there was a stool on which the goalkeeper sat and tried to stop the other side getting the ball under it. Tennis, of a sort, was also popular, and it was an amazing sight to see Douglas Bader playing these games. He may have lacked legs, but his courage was legendary, and without legs he had developed enormously powerful arms and shoulders, which gave him some advantage in these games. Possibly the most *Deutschfeindlich* of all Kriegies, Bader was the sort of man you would follow into the jaws of hell, especially in a Spitfire, but possibly not someone you would have looked to for calm and sober judgement.

Because the courtyard was so confined the Goons had provided a small park outside the castle to which parties were escorted every day. There were still walls and wire and plenty of sentries, but there were also grass and trees and a bit more space. The Goons were asking for trouble by taking Kriegies outside of the main defences of the castle and there were more escapes from, or on the way to, the park than in any other way.

The Goons at Sagan had learned this lesson well; hence the ingenuity needed to get the Delousing Party out through the gate

Not long after we arrived at Colditz I took on the job of running the canteen. We had things to sell, but to understand how the finances worked it is necessary to explain the curious system which operated in the camps. As one of its many unrealistic provisions the Geneva Convention stipulated that officer POWs should receive one third of their pay, whilst other ranks should be paid for the work which they were required to do. Naturally, the Germans were not going to let us have *Reichsmarks*, which were an essential tool for escaping, so they invented a special camp money, known as *Lagergeld* (nothing, alas! to do with beer) and in this currency we were paid, at exchange rate of LM 15 to the £1. The canteen could buy any goods which the Goons would supply and for this purpose could convert *Lagergeld* into *Reichsmarks*. Early in the war, before supplies throughout Germany became very tight, it was possible to buy quite a lot, even including some wine, furniture and musical instruments, but by the time I came about all we could get was newspapers, matches, French cigarettes, near beer (not very near), pencils and paper, and a few oddments which we acquired from time to time. For example, we had a *'Bartbinder'* (a beard binder), whatever that may be, and as may be imagined it was one of our slower moving bits of stock. At Sagan there wasn't much Lagergeld in circulation because we had to support the sergeants in the adjoining compound, who were neither allowed to work nor required to be paid, but there were no NCOs to support at Colditz and the place was awash with *Lagergeld*.

Endless rumours circulated about the ultimate fate of this pseudo money, of which the most optimistic was that after the war it would be converted back into sterling. The pessimists, on the other hand, believed that we would have been docked a third of the pay which was going into our bank accounts in England, while the *Lagergeld* would be worthless. The optimists accumulated vast fortunes in *Lagergeld*, which wasn't difficult because its value for exchange between Kriegies was low, and for gambling lower still, so that people would wager huge sums in this worthless paper. However, a moment's sober reflection told you that the Air Ministry would never contemplate docking our pay on this account any more than it would convert the *Lagergeld* to sterling. Amidst the tumult of war there must have been English and German civil servants busily exchanging data about rates of officers' pay, while the tanks rolled, the bombs burst and the gas chambers swallowed their victims. One day, to my amazement, I was handed a slip of paper by a Goon informing me that I had been promoted to Flight Lieutenant from Acting Flight Lieutenant, and that my pay in *Lagermarks* was increased accordingly, but much good did it do me.

Although there were no spooks at Colditz, there were certainly ghosts and very useful they were too. A 'ghost' was a spare Kriegie whom the Goons didn't know was in the camp, and he was useful because on *Appel* he could cover for someone who, for example, was sealed in and working down a tunnel, or indeed the ghost might be up to some nefarious business himself. Best of all he could be used to conceal the fact that there had been an escape, thus giving the escaper time to get clear. One such ghost was Jack Best, one of Sagan's most eminent escapers, who had lost little time in becoming active when he arrived in Colditz. In April 1943 he went into hiding at the time of someone else's escape and the Goons assumed, as was intended, that he too had escaped and got clear away. He remained a ghost for nearly a year, living in hiding at first, but latterly living normally, apart from not appearing on *Appel*, except when needed. Jack was a ghost with a lively sense of humour, and when he had to sign the book in the canteen for returnable beer bottles, he signed with his *nom de plume* 'J. Balls to You!' Fortunately, the Goons never asked me about this unusual signature, but such was the occasional light relief which came the way of a canteen manager.

By the time I arrived, in August 1943, the Goon defences were becoming more sophisticated, and although there were some further escapes, none got home. In an ancient castle there were countless twists and turns, odd corners and spaces where the measurements didn't seem quite to add up, and this excited an obsessive belief that somewhere there must exist a magic gateway to freedom. Surely somewhere it must be possible to find a secret passage once used by Teutonic knights or clandestine lovers, or to break into a sewer or a hollow wall leading to safety. Surely over the centuries there must have been a need to pass in or out of the castle unobserved, and there certainly was one now, so that all we needed was to find the entrance.

One such possibility was the subject of an escape project code named 'Crown Deep', on which both Lorne and I worked and which centred on a spiral staircase in the northwest corner of the castle in which the spiral turned the wrong way. In mediaeval castles spiral staircases always descended anti-clockwise, so that the defender had his sword arm on the outside, thus putting the attacker at a disadvantage because he would have to wield his sword back-handed. Why then did this staircase in the northwest corner descend clockwise and why was the space at the bottom walled in? We reasoned that if we could get access to this mysterious space something would surely be revealed, and so a way in was cut through the stonework in a cupboard under a window seat on the first floor and a trap door was cast in cement to conceal the entrance.

Lorne and I had the task of maintaining this trap, opening it to let workers in and out and making it undetectable when left closed. This was back to the old Sagan Gadgets Factory business and it was technically as difficult as anything we had

ever done. The problem was that the crack round the edge
of the trap had to be made invisible to the eye of the most
diligent ferret, and the solution finally arrived at was to make
a putty out of Goon soap. This was a substance bearing no
resemblance to real soap, but it served our purpose. It had
to be shaved down into a powder and moistened with water.
Then we sealed the crack with it and scattered stone dust
over everything. The mix was critical. More than a trace of
water and a tell tale line of damp soon showed through the
dust, so that it needed re-dusting, but too little water and the
putty crumbled. However, it wasn't even as simple as that,
as we learned one day when the Goons suddenly swept in for
a search. There was no time to re-dust and Lorne watched in
horror as a ferret opened the cupboard and peered in with a
torch, but lo and behold! the incriminating line vanished
under torch light and all was well.

Crown Deep was discovered later, though probably
through treachery. Kriegies were always neurotic about the
possibility that the Goons might have infiltrated a stool
pigeon, but this time it was for real. On 8 March 1944 a Sub-
Lieutenant Roy Purdy of the RNVR arrived at Colditz and,
being unknown, was put through the usual interrogation at
which it became apparent that his account of himself had
some loose ends. It is never pleasant to accuse someone of
falsehood, not least a fellow prisoner, but eventually it was
decided to confront him, and he soon confessed that he was a
traitor planted by the Goons. The SBO went to the
Kommandant and demanded his immediate removal, refusing
to accept responsibility for his safety if he remained in the
camp. The scene was a bit tense, but two days later Purdy
had gone.

During his brief stay he was thought to have passed Crown
Deep when it was open and to have tipped off the Goons, but
although they searched they never found our trap. Instead,
they drove a hole through the wall at the bottom of the stairs,
and that was the end of Crown Deep. Anyway, we had
discovered nothing which might have led to an escape
passage and the mystery of the wrong handed spiral staircase
remained a mystery. (After the war Purdy, who was indeed a
British officer, was charged with treason, convicted and
sentenced to death, although significantly he was acquitted
on the charge relating to Colditz, so maybe the Goons had
wind of this tunnel from some other evidence. Purdy's

sentence was later commuted to life imprisonment).

By September 1943 the *Oberkommando der Wehrmacht* (The High Command) had issued an order to the effect that damage to the German war economy caused by escapers would lead to their being court martialled instead of the standard couple of weeks in the cooler. The definition of damage to the war economy covered just about everything to do with escaping, including wearing German uniform, so evidently Lorne and I had been lucky only to have been sent to Colditz. By early 1944 the Goons were clamping down really hard on escaping. They were in dire trouble, with their armies in retreat on every sector of the Russian front and in Italy, Allied bombers ranging all over Western Europe by day and by night, and an Allied invasion manifestly imminent. In the circumstances they could ill afford the resources needed to control the Kriegies' favourite pastime and their tempers were understandably growing short. Thus it was that they published the notice 'To all Prisoners of War', which starts off: 'The escape from prison camps is no longer a sport.' What is more, they meant it. In March, when seventy six prisoners went out through the tunnel Harry at Sagan, where a year earlier Lorne and I had installed the ventilation, fifty of them were shot 'while resisting arrest', although in truth they were all murdered in cold blood and on direct orders from Hitler. Inevitably, among them was Roger Bushell, who was a marked man and well knew the risk he was running. With this tragedy something went out of our carefree Kriegie lives, particularly for anyone who had known Sagan. It was enough to put a damper on enthusiasm for escape, and as it became increasingly obvious that the Allies would soon be victorious there seemed less and less point in taking what were now the very serious risks involved.

But for some people escaping was not just a sport. It had become an obsession, or a sacred duty, as it was for Mike Sinclair. Mike had been out several times, but had always been caught. On his seventh attempt he was shot and severely injured and on his eighth he got as far as the Dutch frontier. That was in January 1944. Then, in September, when down in the park, suddenly and without anyone else's foreknowledge, Mike made a dash for it. He had no hope of scaling the wall, but he ignored the shouts of the sentries and was killed by a bullet, which may well not have been aimed to kill, but which by ill chance glanced off his elbow and into his heart. In our minds it was a pointless tragedy, but in his, who knows?

There was one scheme which had been slowly maturing and which, despite the changing attitude to escape, continued right to the end. Back at Sagan, Lorne and I had toyed with the idea of building a glider. Probably it would never have been possible there, but at Colditz the first and only British aircraft manufacturing enterprise in wartime Germany was established by Bill Goldfinch, Jack Best (the 'ghost'), Tony Rolt and 'Stooge' Wardle. But how could you ever build an aircraft in a prison camp? To build a glider you need the design skills, a workshop and tools and then construction skills and materials. Tony Rolt was a soldier, and although Bill and Jack were RAF none of them were aircraft engineers. However, they had Lattimer Needham's early work on aircraft design, which gave sufficient detail of the structure of a simple aircraft to enable them to produce the necessary drawings. The escape committee remained cautious and asked Lorne, who was the only professional aircraft engineer in the camp, to review the design, which he did and pronounced it sound, although he had doubts about the method of launching. However, that was not his responsibility. So far so good, but a workshop concealed from the Goons sounds more difficult. A glider is a biggish thing, but hiding things was a well developed Kriegie skill and the technique used for this workshop was based on what Lorne called the 'positive hole'.

Most holes are made by cutting into something—a hole in the ground or a hole in a wall—and you can use them as hides so long as you can conceal the entrance, but a positive hole is a different and more intellectually subtle concept. You create it out of open space by enclosing it within some structure which was not there before, but which looks as though it was. Thus, in one room there was a buttress on one of the walls, or so it seemed, but it was entirely false and had been built so as to create within it a positive hole. Buttresses were a common feature of the structure of the castle and so this one, which was known as the 'Canary', went unnoticed and provided much useful hiding space. In suitable circumstances a positive hole could be very large, and so it was with the glider workshop. High in the north wing of the castle the top two floors were closed to us. The topmost amounted to little more than a triangular roof space, but it was some seventy feet long, and when a false wall was built across one end the reduction in this long narrow attic was unnoticeable on a casual inspection. Behind the false wall was the workshop, and although the Goons looked in these empty rooms from time to time they never discovered the secret.

The wall was built one Sunday while the band practiced the noisiest music they knew on a floor just below. Shutters from another attic were used and were covered with palliasse covers so that they were like the flats used for stage scenery. Finally, Jack—who had lived in Kenya and so knew about mud huts—coated the fabric with a sort of plaster made from stone dust, which was a by-product of any tunnelling operation. Fortunately, there was no Goon inspection for a week and so the plaster had time to dry. Meantime, a trap door entrance was made in the ceiling of the room below where the plaster had conveniently fallen off the laths so that the trap was inconspicuous.

Apart from the clever design of the positive hole the Goons were deceived because these empty rooms were secured by highly sophisticated locks, so that they had no reason to suppose that we could get in anyway, but they were wrong. The doors in the castle had of course been fitted with locks since time immemorial, but they were primitive things and easily picked, or opened with a skeleton key. The arch lock-manipulator was Bush Parker, an Australian Flight Lieutenant who was also a master of sleight of hand. The ordinary locks yielded to his sensitive fingers as readily as did a pack of cards, and it didn't take the Goons long to realise that they needed better defences against the likes of Bush. So on all the important doors they installed cruciform locks made by Zeiss Ikon, similar to an ordinary Yale lock, but with tumblers on three sides instead of only one. On the face of it they were unbeatable, as no lock picks could possibly be inserted to hold all the tumblers in the open position at the same time. But many desirable things lay behind the locked doors and a determined Kriegie was not to be so easily thwarted. One such was a Dutchman, Van Doorninck, who designed a delicate measuring instrument which could be inserted into the lock to measure the movement of each tumbler in turn, so that when all the dimensions were known a key could easily be made. This was precision engineering at its best and a triumph of ingenuity, which can still be seen in the museum at Colditz.

The glider itself needed only simple carpentry, some wood, one or two bed sheets, and glue, all of which could be found somewhere in the castle. Timber for the the main structural members, like wing spars and struts, was from floor boards, while lighter parts used wood from furniture such as cupboards, which often have plywood backs. Boards of the length and quality needed for spars were found in the *Saalhaus*, which was inhabited by senior officers, and were replaced by shorter pieces from an inconspicuous corner elsewhere. The *Saalhaus* was on the opposite side of the courtyard from the workshop, so some tricky work was needed to do the swap. The short boards were nailed to a table to look like its usual top. That could be carried openly, but for the long pieces there was nothing for it but to rush them across while no Goon was looking.

Glue was another problem. Condensed milk might have been used for the lightly stressed parts, but fortunately a supply of the real thing was obtained through the usual subversive methods. The wings and fuselage were clad with material from palliasse covers, which was not so different from the fabric normally used in those days. It had a pretty blue and white check so the glider looked very handsome. In addition to the four main participants many sub-contractors worked on this great enterprise. Components such as spars and wing ribs were made before the workshop was completed and were hidden under a floor. I did some work on these and once went up to the workshop. It was an uncanny experience, first of all slipping into the locked room below, while the stooges kept careful watch. Then up through the trap into this big positive hole, looking for all the world like the workshop at Cambridge, where I helped to build a glider for the Club.

Because the glider was not finished until nearly the end of the war it was never flown, and so what looked like a chancy launch procedure was never put to the test. It involved taking the aircraft out and rigging it on the sloping roof from which a long wooden spar would project with a rope from the aircraft, round a pulley at the end and then back inside the castle to a heavy weight. On the word go this would be dropped through a hole cut in the floor, and so catapult the glider into the air. Fortunately, the roof was shielded from the floodlights so the preparations could be undetected. At the time there were frequent air raids demanding complete blackout, and that would have been the ideal moment to launch. It may sound dodgy, but like the aircraft itself it had all been carefully thought out, as can be seen from a page of Bill's calculations in Appendix C.

Brilliant as the glider project was, it involved a vast investment of time, ingenuity and materials for the possibility of only two people getting out, for which reason it was criticized by some, although it always had official support and it was certainly therapeutic in that it gave an objective which many people could work for. Anyway, the war might well not have ended when and how it did and the glider might yet have proved a life-saver.

But just as brilliant were schemes derived from someone's inspiration in spotting a weakness in the Goon defences which could be exploited quickly and with a minimum of effort. Such a one was devised by John Beaumont, who was a regular Army officer and had been taken prisoner on the retreat to Dunkirk. Later, in the camp at Eichstatt, he had escaped through a tunnel with sixty-four others and headed, as most of them did, for Switzerland, 130 miles away. To reach the frontier they would have to cross the Danube, but with such a *Massenflucht* all the bridges would have been closely guarded. John started to build a raft, but was caught in the process and taken to prison in Augsburg, where he found some of the others. It was a Gestapo prison, which boded ill, but fortunately the *Wehrmacht* traced them there and, being determined to protect its own prisoners, got them out of the hands of the Gestapo and back to Eichstatt. They were still not out of trouble, for higher authority was furious, and after a few days they were marched to the old castle outside Eichstatt, along roads lined by SS guards with machine guns. There they were lodged in the dungeons until a fortnight later all sixty five were sent to Colditz, where they arrived in June 1943.

John had been a prisoner for four years, which was more than enough, and there had been so many escapes from Colditz that it was now difficult to find a way out which had not been blocked. He searched and schemed, until suddenly he realised that if he turned himself into a pile of rubbish he might get out. The path down to the park passed close along the outside wall of the castle; it was a narrow path with, at

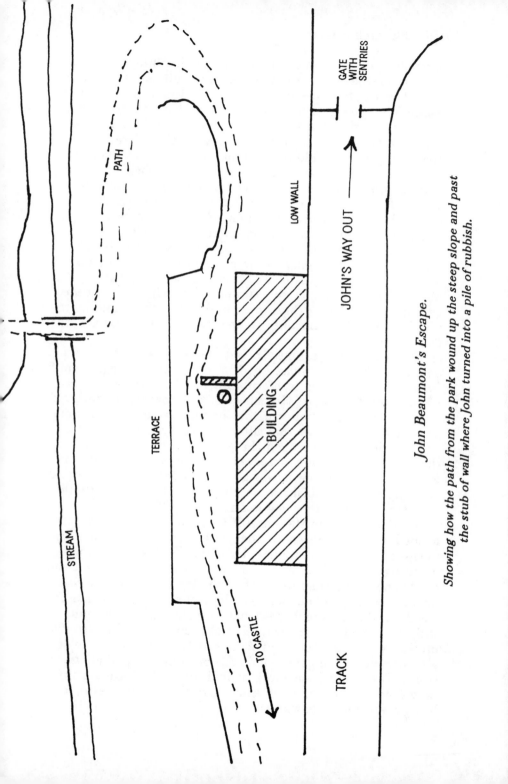

John Beaumont's Escape.

Showing how the path from the park wound up the steep slope and past the stub of wall where John turned into a pile of rubbish.

Labels within the diagram: STREAM, PATH, TERRACE, TO CASTLE, BUILDING, LOW WALL, TRACK, JOHN'S WAY OUT, GATE WITH SENTRIES one point, a stub of wooden fence projecting into it. John saw that, if as the party returned up the hill he were to slip behind the uphill side of this stub, he would be behind the back of the guard in front while it would need only a minor diversion for the guard at the rear not to see him disappear. Then, if he turned into a pile of rubbish before the rear guard passed, he would be invisible. It would only remain for his absence to be covered at the count when the party reached the entrance to the castle, and then as soon as the coast was clear he could slip quietly away. He made a cloak to which he attached a selection of old tins, bits of paper, twigs, leaves and so on, and spent time practicing collapsing neatly under it so that he was completely covered. It was May 1944 and still chilly, so he planned to conceal this cloak under a capacious greatcoat. Then, as we came back up the hill we would pack closely round him, with taller people behind, thus allowing him to duck out of sight, while at the critical moment someone at the rear would distract the guard's attention.

Those were the essentials, but there were two important details: the rear guard had a dog, which might sniff suspiciously at the pile of rubbish, so John smeared garlic liberally on his cloak. He had been told that garlic deterred dogs just as Lorne believed that pepper would do the same. The next hazard was that after the party had left a Goon with a dog always searched the park and then came back up the same path. John observed him for several weeks and found that on average it was seven minutes before he would pass the pile of rubbish, so he planned to be gone in the few minutes before another dog might come sniffing around.

For those of us in the know it was a bit edgy as the party formed up to go down to the park. So many people had escaped from park parties that the Goons were forever counting us, but John survived the count, first as we left the castle and again when we reached the bottom. Then he had a nerve-racking two hour wait for the return and his chance for freedom, during which he could only bite his nails, put up with the smell of garlic and make sure that his strange undergarment stayed out of sight. At last the time came and we gathered at the gate, only a few of us knowing what was in store. Being tall I was close behind him. We jostled a little as we passed the stub of fence and then, hey presto, one Kriegie vanished into thin air.

When he got up to go John found to his horror that the Goon with the dog had cut short his search of the park and was already starting up the path, so he scrambled back under his rubbish. He lay quaking and hoping that his feet were not sticking out, but maybe it was true about the garlic for the Goon and his dog passed safely. Now, dressed as a civilian, John got away, held his breath as he passed a gate with unexpected sentries and reached the road east of the castle. Full of hope he started the sixty mile trek to Czechoslovakia where he had been told of a safe house, at which he must give the password 'Nerodil' to a priest.

The rest of us carried on to the castle, where the count was successfully fudged. Then came the agonising wait to see whether the next thing would be a discreet message from England or—more likely—that he would soon turn up in the cooler. Worst of all, and only too likely in view of that message 'To all Prisoners of War', would be a polite word from the Kommandant: 'I am sorry, but Lieutenant Beaumont, who despite explicit warnings, was foolish enough to leave the protection of the castle, has been shot while resisting arrest.' As it was, we did not have to wait long, for he was picked up almost immediately while walking along the road and was back in the cooler for the regulation fourteen days solitary. Perhaps he had been lucky, because in fact the safe house had already been blown.

Like everyone else, Kriegies liked a drink now and again. Wine of sorts could be made with raisins and a bit of extra sugar, and with luck there was enough yeast left on the raisins to get the fermentation going, but supplies were limited. Then a bit of brilliant lateral thinking produced a breakthrough and the production of alcohol became a growth industry based on an ample supply of raw material and some ingenious technology. The material was what the Goons called jam, although it was barely recognisable as such. They issued quite a substantial ration of the stuff, but it was so disgusting that few people ate it. It was a pulpy substance, dyed a hideous purple and artificially flavoured. Perhaps it was a by-product of sugar beet refining, but anyway someone realised that as it did contain a small proportion of sugar it should be possible to ferment it, which indeed it was. Because no one wanted it on their bread it was not difficult to collect large quantities ('Could I have your jam ration, old boy?'), and soon whole *Kübels* full could be seen going 'glug, glug', like boiling mud, and emitting a revolting smell. Of course, you could not drink the mush, but you could distil it and witches—or maybe they were alchemists—were to be seen bending over their seething cauldrons and jealously guarding the precious fluid as it dripped from the improvised stills. It was 'jam alc', once tasted never to be forgotten—and deadly. It could be improved by filtering with charcoal, obtained from medical supplies, and arguably it could be further improved by adding powdered milk and sugar, but by any standards it was disgusting.

Disgusting or not, many people acquired a taste for it and the demand for Reich jam soon exceeded the ration. However, alcoholics are nothing if not cunning and very soon an operation was mounted to raid the cellar where barrels of the stuff were stored. The lock on the cellar door was a simple one and scarcely merited Bush Parker's tender touch, but the entrance was in the courtyard, and so some careful Goon watching and diversion were necessary so as to slip in and out without being seen. The same cellar contained potatoes, and some time later when food was scarce I was on a potato raiding party which went wrong and we ended up in the cooler for a week. It was winter and miserably cold, the one source of light or heat in the cell being a forty watt bulb. About the only diversion from the discomfort was air raid warnings, and one night when we were all taken down to a shelter Bush, who had been with us to open the cellar door, produced a pack of cards with which he proceeded to play card tricks. The guard with us in the shelter was a simple soul and looked as though he suspected black magic, almost cowering in a corner when Bush invited him to 'pick a card'.

Ever since the beginning Kriegies had been saying "Home by Christmas" and "We won't see another Christmas in the *schaft*". (*Gefangenschaft*—captivity.) But as the years went by this wore a bit thin and some wit was heard to say: "Home or homo by Christmas," although actually homosexuality was rare. More to the point, it dawned on us that 1944 would be a leap year and it was for sure that we would not see another leap year in the *schaft*. This meant that 29 February 1944 must be the occasion for an almighty bash, and for months beforehand the stills worked overtime, while the stocks of jam alc steadily grew, some of them being recorded on giant thermometers which more usually show the amount collected for the repair of the church roof. Came the night and scenes of orgy were everywhere, while next day there were many who were very, very ill, although surprisingly no one actually died. Not everything on offer was necessarily jam alc though and there was one little gem of a scene when 'Scarlet' O'Hara, already very drunk, was handed another glass. Scarlet was a hard drinking Irishman and he was not too drunk to smell a rat. He sniffed the glass, then solemnly threw the contents over a table, held his cigarette lighter to it and watched as the table erupted into flames. Meths probably, or surgical spirit. The Goons seemed to take the view that it was none of their business if Englishmen chose to poison themselves, but the stills did not always escape arrest, and there was one sad occasion when we were all in the courtyard while a major search was in progress and one of them was carried out, still spouting steam and accompanied by cries of protest.

There was no shortage of activities in Colditz in addition to escaping and brewing booze. On arrival I had turned down an offer to start again in the theatre, but by mid 1944 I had given up the canteen and went back to the stage. *Hay Fever* again, Coward's *Tonight at Eight Thirty* and Cronin's *Jupiter Laughs.* I even started to adapt a book of Somerset Maugham's for the stage, but this enterprise was overtaken by the end of the war, which was probably just as well. I also made props for the theatre, an innocent form of Gadget Factory work. Another worker in this field was George Drew who, with Hamish Hamilton, from the Eichstatt tunnel, ran the 'Tatty Box Company' and built scenery, which was painted by John Watton. John was a talented painter and drew many portraits of the inmates, including the frontispiece to this book. George had a little workshop where he also spent much of his time wood carving and where he produced his masterpiece, a set of chess men in which the pieces were either characters from *Alice in Wonderland* or caricatures of camp personalities. He still has it. The chisels with which he carved the set—and which he still uses—I made for him out of broken fencing swords, learning in the process how to soften and temper tool steel.

Why we were allowed to have such swords is a mystery. They could just as easily have been fashioned into daggers. George carved these chess men in a few weeks near the end of the war and says that it was all that kept him sane in those difficult days while we were waiting for the end.

Dating from one of its previous occupations the castle had a proper theatre and stage which made it possible to put on productions for which we could build splendid sets, but which were always bedevilled by poor lighting. One of the standing jokes was the stage direction in a play which specified '5000 watts on the crazy paving', but alas, 500 watts was more likely the most we could muster. To try to improve things I set out to make a spotlight, and after some study of the principles of parabolic reflectors managed to produce a formidable instrument which was dubbed the 'PIAT', after the weapon known as the Projector Infantry Anti-Tank. It did not do much to improve the lighting, but making it was a lot of fun. Anyway, we put on plenty of good entertainment and as at Sagan it was enjoyed by Goon officers as much as by Kriegies.

Another pastime, practiced by a select few, was making telescopes. They were commonly known as 'lechoscopes', since one of their uses was to observe the antics of the locals among the bushes in the surrounding countryside. It is not all that difficult to grind a lens out of a piece of perspex and formidable magnifications were achieved. The technology was crude and the scopes were not only enormously long, but the image was surounded by a blaze of all the colours in the spectrum, adding a spectacular effect to some of the activities observed. A more refined art was practiced by a friend who designed and made horns. I had a gramophone—goodness knows where it came from; it just turned up one day in a parcel without any indication of the sender. We fitted a gigantic horn to this machine which then had fantastic acoustics in which every note seemed to emerge separately. It was known as the 'Winklehorn'.

Many people played bridge, but if you were not yourself a bridge player and could not get away from the incessant patter of 'Two, no Trumps,' etc, it could seriously damage your health. One person who found not only this, but any other mindless chatter too much for him, was 'Skipper' Barnett. Skipper, a gnarled little man, would have been happier in a monastery than in a prison camp, and to make the best of a bad job he spent much of his time living cross legged on the top of a tall locker. There he would ingest enormous quantities of air until such time as he could bear his fellow men no more, when he would expel it in a formidable fart which went on for minutes. It was a telling way of expressing his disapproval. It may also have contributed to his yoga exercises whereby he contrived artificially to raise his blood pressure to such a degree that he was able to persuade the Goons that he was so ill that he should be repatriated. He was one of a very few who carried off this deception and he went home with one or two more who were genuinely very sick. Another phoney condition which was tried was the so-called 'wire psychosis', but the trouble with that was that if you spent long enough feigning mental instability you were liable to end up genuinely crazy.

In an act of imagination The Royal Yachting Association had offered a prize of fifty pounds (a decent sum in those days) for the best design of a cruising yacht by a prisoner of war, and Lorne went in for it. When in a creative mood Lorne of course needed his usual 'ignorant bystander' to criticize his efforts, not to mention holding his tools. We had a lot of fun doing this, making the best of the lack of proper drawing facilities and mocking up bits of cabin and cockpit with the help of beds and chairs and anything else which would help us see whether what was on the drawing board would fit in real life. Lorne won the prize, but sadly the boat was never built.

As 1944 wore on the plight of the German armies became more and more desperate on every front, including in the west after the Allies had landed in Normandy. The RAF and the American Air Force were devastating the country with ever increasing ferocity and air raids on targets near Colditz became common. A dozen miles away there were synthetic oil and chemical plants which were frequently attacked, and even at that distance the noise of exploding bombs was horrendous enough to give a taste of what it must be like to be on the receiving end. At night there were volcanic eruptions of flame while searchlights criss-crossed a sky flickering with bursting flak. All this gave a boost to our morale. One night there was an air raid warning and a few aircraft could be heard high overhead. Then suddenly the sky was ablaze with flares drifting slowly down on their parachutes, lighting up the castle and the town. We rushed to the windows and moments later came the all enveloping roar of a thousand Merlins driving the main bomber force high overhead. The Pathfinders had marked Colditz with their flares, but Good God! surely this sleepy little country town could not be the target, or had they made a ghastly mistake and were we about to be blown to pieces? As usual during an air raid warning the castle floodlights were out; everyone crowded at the windows and the sentries, unable to take cover, and edgy because of possible escapes in the dark, were shouting with a rising note of hysteria: *"Zurück vom Fenster oder wird erschossen!"* The roar of the Lancasters and Halifaxes rose to a crescendo, but Colditz can only have been marked as a turning point on the route for soon it died away without any bombs raining down. The aircraft had gone on their way to the target and our hearts went with them.

By day great fleets of American Flying Fortresses would drone relentlessly across the sky while fighters, both Luftwaffe and escorts, weaved in and out. Often the vapour trails would spread out into a continuous sheet of cloud, interspersed with an occasional smoke trail where some one had fallen prey to a Messerschmitt or a Focke-Wulf. Those of us who had been up there wondered how anyone could have the courage sit for hour after hour in broad daylight waiting to be shot at, and probably not having to wait very long.

On 13 June, 1944, the first Flying Bombs fell on London. The Germans knew them as the V1, V standing for *Vergeltungswaffe* or 'Revenge Weapon'. It was four days before what was intended both to destroy the will of the British civil population and restore flagging German morale was reported. Then the German papers came out with lurid headlines about the damage done. The *Volkischer Beobachter* of 17 June was headed *'MIT NEUEN SPRENGKORPERN GROSS-TENS KALIBERS GEGEN LONDON UND SUDENGLAND'* ('With new expolosive devices of the largest calibre against London and South England'), but we had the BBC news and knew that it was not as serious as the Germans made out. Part of the original script of the one o'clock news of 16 June appears opposite. On 8 September the first V2 rockets fell, about which we were equally relaxed, although little did we know that had it not been for a bad decision by Hitler the V2 might well have been carrying an atomic war head and would have been a real *Vergeltungswaffe*. The V weapons did little to restore German morale and there was a growing acceptance, anyway among the guards, that the end could not be far away. Perhaps it was best exemplified by little

Here is the news read by ALVAR LIDELL.

No big change in Normandy is reported this morning, but some progress has been made in the drive across the Cherbourg Peninsula. All enemy counter-attacks have been repulsed, and our striking power is still increasing. Last night, R.A.F. heavy bombers were out in great strength against E-Boats and minesweepers in Boulogne Harbour.

The enemy has started using pilot-less aircraft against this country. A few were over southern England in the early hours of Tuesday morning, and more were over last night and this morning. Mr. Herbert Morrison has made a statement about them in Parliament.

Advances of up to twenty-five miles were made by our troops in Italy yesterday. We now hold Terni, and have pushed ten miles beyond Orvieto.

The new super-Fortresses which attacked Tokyo came from the China-Burma Theatre. New details about these aircraft have come from our Washington correspondent. American troops have landed on Saipan, in the Mariana Islands.

The Russians have broken through a second Finnish defence-zone in the Karelian Isthmus.

T. WINTER

BBC New Bulletin.

The actual script from which Alvar Lidell read the One O'clock News on 16 June, 1944, telling of the first flying bombs. To protect against enemy propaganda broadcasts being mistaken for the BBC it had become the practice to name the news readers so as to help listeners recognise them.

Willi Pohnert, a civilian electrician who looked after the installations in the castle and a man resigned to his fate as one on whom the world wipes its feet. One day I said to him:

"Well Willi, when the war is over what is going to become of you?"

The V weapons were much in the news at the time, and after he had reflected for a moment he replied:

"Ah *Herr* Morison, I think I shall become *Vergeltungs-mittel* [material for revenge]."

In fact, Willi did rather better than that, and despite being in the Russian sector he was alive and well and looking reasonably prosperous many years later when some old inmates visited Colditz.

In May 1944 a Frenchman, Tony du Puy, arrived in the camp, and not long afterwards my mess invited him to dinner. At that time we still had plenty of Red Cross parcels and could provide a decent meal, by Kriegie standards anyway, though no doubt not quite what he was accustomed to at home. He lived on the Loire where he farmed his estates at Saumur and was the local Count. I was rather pleased with my cullinary efforts and gave my mother the recipe for the prune tart which was served:

Take about a pound and a half of barley [we never had wheat] *and grind to a very coarse meal in a sort of mincing machine (Brown & Poulson's flour might be preferable). Mix with fat, sugar and salt and bake into an open tart. Allow to cool. Take six ounces of butter and six of sugar and whip for about an hour, or preferably get someone else to whip it. Stew, stone and mash about 25 prunes, add to butter and whip a bit more. Add the resulting mixture, which is both gastronomically and aesthetically extremely satisfying, to the center of the tart. Crack the prune stones and sprinkle the kernels over all. Cut so that one slice is definitely, but not too noticeably bigger than the rest and serve.—sufficient for eight. You should try it some day.*

Such had been the daily round of life at Colditz, often dull, sometimes dramatic, mostly fairly comfortable, but soon it was to change as the final act began to unfold.

CHAPTER TEN

The End at Last

IN May 1944 it had been dinner parties with prune tart—but by October we were on half parcels, although not seriously hungry.

However, life steadily became more tedious as we waited wearily for the end which, although now inevitable, seemed unconscionably slow in coming. With escaping no longer a worthwhile pursuit and no clear purpose other than to survive until an unpredictable, but possibly traumatic liberation, our morale sank or fluctuated wildly according to the progress of the Allied armies. We became edgy as we speculated on how the end would come. Would it be the Russians, with the Goons moving us away as they approached? It was winter and the prospect was daunting. Might the Goons turn nasty and use us as *Vergeltungs-mittel*? It seemed all too likely. If they did, would we resist and if so, how? That they might turn nasty was indeed a possibility, as Miles Reid recounted in his book *Into Colditz*:

When he was first a prisoner in Greece in 1941 there was a civilian visitor to his camp whom Miles recognised as a German who before the war had lived in Hollywood. There he had been in an anti-Nazi brawl, and had acquired a conspicuous scar on his forehead and was also conspicuous by the camelhair coat which he wore. He was from the German Foreign Office and they got to know one another a little, but he faded from Miles' mind until in the Autumn of 1944, when the scene shifted to the courtyard at Colditz and Miles suddenly saw the same scar and camel coat. Recognition was mutual, and after a few words they retired discreetly to Miles' room, where the German confided that he was still with the Foreign Office and that his mission to Colditz was to gauge the likely response should an order be received that certain prisoners—doubtless the Prominente—were to be shot.

He said that the report which he would be delivering to Berlin would be that in his judgement the order would not be obeyed. Although at first sight that may seem to have been good news it showed which way the wind was blowing. Anyway, if the Kommandant disobeyed the order the likely consequence would be that someone more ruthless would take over and the Kommandant would be shot first with the Prominente soon after. This disquieting news was known only to a few senior officers, which was just as well.

By Christmas 1944 we were still eating reasonably well, but with Germany, and in particular its transport system, dissolving into chaos the supply of parcels soon dwindled. At the same time the Goons were evacuating prisoners eastwards before the advancing Allied armies in the west. They had to put them somewhere and many were crammed into Colditz. By March our numbers had risen from three hundred to two thousand, and all this in a castle which was clearly inelastic. These newcomers arrived with whatever posessions they could carry, or push in improvised hand carts. Many of them were French and among them was Pierre de Vomécourt, who had first been parachuted into France in 1941 to work with the Resistance. After capture he had somehow escaped the firing squad, but needless to say that was not something which he would talk about. From the east came Poland's General Bor-Komorowski who, when the Russians were only a few miles distant, had led the tragic uprising of the Warsaw Poles against the Germans. Stalin did not want a lot of fiercely independent Poles on his doorstep and cynically held back his army until the Germans had done his dirty work by massacring most of the insurgents. The General was a Prominenter among Prominente, and his enduring influence among his countrymen was such as to bring several visits from high ranking Germans. They tried to seduce him with promises of freedom if he would raise a Polish army to fight the Russians. They should have known better: the Poles prized their honour above all else and the offers were contemptuously refused.

We were now short of food; not starving, but hungry, then very hungry. So hungry, indeed, that at one time I was collecting turnip peelings thrown out by the cookhouse and peeling them again to get a little extra. A few parcels arrived, some from Switzerland and some from Denmark, which reputedly we owed to the relationship of one of the Prominente to the Danish Royal Family. With so many people in the camp they did not go far, and there were disputes between different nationalities as to whom the parcels belonged.

The winter was cold, we were hungry and we were overcrowded, but we stayed healthy, although some who had been prisoners for five years were looking a bit ragged at the edges. To care for our health we had no less than three doctors, a dentist and even a dental surgery, left over from pre-war days. Eric Cooper was fully employed, doing over fifteen hundred fillings and five hundred extractions and complaining that every filling hurt him more than the patient because of an electrical fault in his drill which gave him a shock every time he used it. There was Dr Dickie from England, Dr Moody from New Zealand—known as 'Birdikin' Moody—and Dr Draffin from Ireland, known as the 'Bog Doctor' or 'Bog *Arzt*' and renowned for his eccentricity. He even tried to extract the poison from a wasp sting on my arm by using a hypodermic in reverse.

The doctors had medicines from the Red Cross, even including some of the new sulpha drugs, which certainly saved the life of at least one Kriegie with an acute lung infection. They had also managed to accumulate reserve stocks of tea which they would issue from time to time when morale was particularly low. It had an instantly soothing effect on the nerves and they claimed a significant drop in attendance at surgery as a result. We also had three priests, C of E, Methodist and Roman Catholic. It seems unlikely that so many doctors and priests can have been fiercely *Deutschfeindlich*, so perhaps the Goons thought we were in special need of bodily and spiritual care. For the latter we also had an imposing crucifix, known as 'INRI', who lived in INRI's cupboard, up by the theatre. We knew that was his name because it was written on him!

The last letter which I wrote home—or anyway the last to make it through the mounting chaos—was dated 26 March, and in it I appeared cheerful:

Perfect spring weather has arrived and yesterday I was sunbathing in the courtyard with my shirt off, though with 2000 people in the camp it loses some of its attraction. Things being what they are spirits (and the smell) are pretty high.

The 'things' in question were that the German armies were collapsing and the Allies were only a hundred and fifty miles from Colditz. Not long ago my comments would have been censored, but the Goons had ceased to care. My letter home may have looked cheerful—it had to—but we were torn between elation and apprehension as to how it would all end. We ordinary Kriegies may have had our worries, mostly kept to ourselves, but who would have wanted the burden carried by the Senior British Officer, Colonel Tod, on whose handling of the situation everyone's safety would depend when the final crunch came?   On 11 April we knew from the radio that the fighting was close, and Willy Tod chose that moment to go to the Kommandant and demand to know his intentions.   The reply which he got was ominous, for it was that the Kommandant awaited orders from Himmler, the notorious head of the SS.   However, the Kommandant had as much cause to worry as we, for if he failed to deliver us safely into the hands of the Allies the outlook for him would be bleak, yet he could still be shot out of hand if he disobeyed an order from his superiors.   It would be a delicate negotiation in which each must be seen to fight for his own side while both knew that they desired the same outcome.

In the town below the castle we could see troops mining the bridge over the Mulde, and that spelt trouble.   There were SS in the area who evidently intended to hold the line of the river, in which event we would be in the middle of a battle, although as *Hauptmann* Eggers, one of the camp officers, wrote in his diary: "God knows what they think they are still fighting for."

On the 14th, when we could hear distant gunfire, the SS commander came to the castle and demanded reinforcements from the guards, but the Kommandant persuaded him that all his men were old and had few weapons, and that it would be safer to leave them to guard the castle rather than risk having two thousand POWs on the rampage as the Americans approached.   It was crucial to stop the SS occupying the castle for defence, to which they agreed, but stipulated that if white or national flags were displayed we would instantly be shelled.   The trouble for us was that if we did not identify ourselves we were just as likely to be shelled by the Americans.

Later on the same day the Kommandant received orders to destroy all records and evacuate the prisoners towards the east.   This was the crunch.   If we stayed in the castle under the protection of the German officers, who knew that their interest was to hand us over to the Americans, we would be relatively safe and could expect to be relieved within a day or two; but if we started marching about in the chaotic conditions prevailing between the Russian and American forces anything could happen. The SBO, together with the senior French and American officers, flatly refused to budge, saying that there would be violent resistance if the Germans tried to force us out of the castle. The Kommandant, who had learned that when Willy Tod said something he meant it, phoned the area High Command. There was much discussion. We remained adamant. There was more phoning, but we kept up the pressure until it was agreed that we should stay put. Then, with impeccable timing, Colonel Tod, who was recognised by the others as the senior Allied officer, demanded, and got, the Kommandant's surrender and the keys of the castle.

Little did we know of the tense scenes which had been enacted in the *Kommandantur*, but we knew that Willy Tod had scored a great victory. So far so good, but still anything could happen. The SS might well turn nasty. If they came into the castle we would be trapped and they were not likely to be gentle. If they shelled us the five foot thick walls would not stop anti-tank shells and the place would likely burn down. Now came the sound of machine gun fire from up the hill; were they taking a last chance to shoot the Jews in the concentration camp there? Alas, probably yes. Would they soon be shooting us? It seemed all too likely. But despite these nagging worries the excitement and the drama were intense, for within a few hours we would be free—or dead.

We did not know exactly what was happening, but in fact an American force which was heading for Leipzig had received orders to send a detachment to Colditz, where there were said to be prisoners of war, including VIPs. There had indeed been VIPs, but only days previously the Prominente had been taken away. The SBO had resisted fiercely, but the Goons were adamant and not surprisingly because, as we learned later, they had a letter signed by Hitler ordering the Prominente to be taken to his Last Redoubt in Bavaria. It stated that anyone allowing them to fall into Allied hands would be shot. On their journey towards Bavaria they had hair raising adventures, but in the end the responsible officer realised on which side his bread was buttered and handed them over to the Swiss, Hitler's letter being given to a British officer.

Next day, the 15th, the Yanks came within range and battle
raged all day. Shells started to fall on the town and the SS,
who were on the high ground behind us, fired back. Soon
shells were screeching to and fro over our heads. The SS
tried to blow the bridge, but there was only a feeble 'crump',
and not much damage. Next morning, as the fighting
continued, we could see GIs moving through the town and
mopping up. There were white flags everywhere until they
came to one house where there was some resistance. In a
moment a couple of shells were called down on it, a white
bedsheet fluttered out and the GIs moved on. They certainly
were not wasting time on niceties.

One or two shells hit the castle. Douglas Bader was knock-
ed off his tin legs, but no one was hurt. The time had come
to identify ourselves. The SS threat about flags was still real,
but there were American aircraft overhead so we laid out big
British and French flags in the courtyard where the SS could
not see them. The Pongo prisoners were watching the battle
with professional interest, but it was getting too hot for me.
The time had come to try and ensure surviving the last hours
of the war, so I crept away to hide under the stairs as far from
the gunfire as possible. I was ashamed of being so scared,
but in the same refuge I found Tommy Catlow and Douglas
Bader, in no better shape. I had always admired submariners
as the bravest of the brave, so with him and a legless fighter
ace for company I felt a little better.

Soon it was over. The great wooden doors, of which for so
long we had seen only the wrong side, swung open and the
Yanks were in the courtyard. Their tanks seemed to be
dripping with Grand Marnier—'Hey fella, take a swig of this.'
Everything was a whirl, a dream. The glider was brought out
and rigged for all to see, including the astonished Goons.
Alas! later efforts to bring it home were frustrated by the
Russians who occupied the area. The French, who had a
sense of occasion, were called out on parade and were
addressed by their senior officer: *"Les Messieurs Français,
Prisoniers de Guerre pas encore."* I don't remember if they
played the *Marseillaise*. Life was too confused to take it all in.
We wandered through the *Kommandantur* picking up
anything of interest, but the only thing I came away with was
a confiscated skeleton key. We would not be able to carry
much home and hadn't anything to pack it in anyway so I
went to the cookhouse and took one of the magnificent *Kübels*,

which served as a carrier as well as a trophy. It was a wise choice and I still use it. Lorne was more relaxed. He went out for a walk, picked rhubarb in a garden, and had a good look at the castle from the outside.

Early next day we were loaded into lorries and set off, but the Yanks who had rescued us were way out in front of their main forces and we were not out of the wood yet. Well, actually, we were in a wood when the column halted, paused, turned back and took another road. The problem? There was a German tank just round the corner. Germany was still a dangerous place. Eventually we reached the Luftwaffe airfield at Kölleda, from where we would be flown home. This was a big supply base, and as there was some time to wait we wandered round the hangars looking for something to liberate. Two thousand horsepower aero engines were going for free, but anything both useful and portable was scarce and in the end all I took was a screwdriver. Lorne did better. He liberated two parachute bags, which he still uses. He was sad to leave some magnificent field glasses on a tripod, but could not carry them.

Then we climbed into a fleet of US Air Force Dakotas and were airborne once again. Some of us turned a bit green. Were they the ones who had so confidently stood in the windows watching the battle while I cowered under the stairs? Tommy Catlow was there, scared that he would be shot down once again—and who would blame him? Lorne was in the same aircraft. It was not quite the same as if we had made it in the Junkers, but we didn't care. We asked the gum-chewing pilot where we were going and were introduced to a novel style of navigation: "Just followin' da' guy in front, ain't I." Slowly the Third and Last Reich slipped away behind us for ever. We stopped briefly at Liège, then Brussels and finally landed at Westcot, in Oxfordshire, where we were given a WAAF each to guide us through the proceedures. They were the first women we had spoken to for three years. Later I can remember being smothered in DDT powder, a real delousing party if ever there was one.

It was late in the day when we landed at Westcott and we had come a long way from the Schloss overlooking the sleepy little country town on the banks of the Mulde, whose now bewildered people had been friendly enough whenever we had any contact with them, and where our guards had carried out their duties honourably. But our journey was not yet over. That evening we were loaded into a train which rattled its way through the night to Cosford, near Wolver-hampton, where at long last I found myself again in an RAF mess, eating eggs and bacon in the small hours of the morning, for all the world as though I had made it safely back from Essen those many months before. Lorne went to his room after eating his bacon and eggs, found a bathroom with lots of hot water, then put on the new pyjamas and dressing gown laid out on his bed, and returned to the mess for more bacon and eggs. This raised a few eyebrows from the regular inhabitants who were now having their normal breakfast, but there was no rebuke.

We were home, but sadly we had left behind the fifty who went out through the tunnel Harry, and were shot, and would never come home.

Aftermath

COSFORD was not an airfield, but a dreary place where we went through tedious procedures. We had medical examinations. We were sent on leave. We were recalled. We had tests. The war in Europe was now virtually over, but there was still very much a war on with Japan and we wondered whether we would have to serve there. It seemed unlikely, although it was not until 5 August that the atom bomb finally answered that question. We were sent on leave again. Everyone was terribly kind but there wasn't anything much to do. Nearly all my friends from the pre-Kriegie days were dead and life was in limbo. Then one day the phone rang and it was Lorne:

"Walter? How are you?"

"Fine, how are you?"

"Fine; but look, if I stay at home a day longer I shall go mad."

"Same here. Where can we go?"

"I think we might be able to get a boat on the Norfolk Broads."

"Great idea. See if you can fix it."

So we hired the 'Wood Anenome', all lovingly varnished mahogany, shining and beautiful, and we sailed out of Ludham to drift care-free around the Broads for three weeks of perfect peace, almost the only boat on the water. The people of Norfolk had been kind hosts to the RAF and to the American airmen through years of suffering and we only had to go into a waterside pub and murmur the words 'RAF' and 'POW' and beers would be pressed into our hands by these good people.

This happy interlude on the water had to end, and then it was back to Cosford, but still there was nothing serious for us to do. Naturally, I fell in love with a WAAF, but that was not a full time occupation. I was selected to represent returned POWs at a Buckingham Palace Garden Party, but that turned out to be scarcely the vision of freedom that I had dreamed of in Colditz. However, there was one old friend who was still around and that was Derek Bolton, with whom I had stood beside the letter box in Cheam in September 1939 and taken a deep breath as we slipped in our applications to join the RAF. He was now Wing Commander Bolton and was with his Lancaster squadron at Wyton, which was not too far from Cosford, so with the help of yet more leave, I went on a visit. Derek took me flying in a Proctor and an Oxford, and I was thrilled to find that I still had the touch and could do a passable take off and landing. For the people on the squadron at Wyton, just as much as for returned prisoners of war at Cosford, life was all anti-climax with nothing of any importance left to do. To keep the boys a bit busy Derek had them flying 'Cook's Tours', on which ground crews and other deserving cases were taken to see the mess which they had been helping to make in Germany. On one of these trips I flew the Lanc at low level round what was once the great industrial area of the Ruhr, Bomber Command's 'Happy Valley'. We flew over those places whose chilling names had come up day after day at briefings on a hundred bomber stations, but which the crews had seen only dimly through the blaze of flares and fires and searchlights: Essen, Hamm, Duisburg, Dortmund, Düsseldorf. Now the flak was silent, but not only the flak. Over the whole area there was utter desolation; not a chimney smoked, no train, nor lorry, nor human being could be seen to move. It had been total war.

Back at Cosford I was soon demobilised, and that day, for the first time in many years, I wept. For five years I had ruthlessly repressed all emotion; and now at the loss of an old love it had to start coming out. But it was no use crying; some sort of new life had to be started—but what?   At Colditz I had pursued my accountancy studies with some diligence, even taking—and, surprisingly enough, passing—an examination of The Institute of Book-keepers, but it had gradually dawned on me that there could be no more dismal way of spending the rest of my life than as an accountant. I had decided instead to go into civil aviation and so switched my studies to navigation and meteorology. I wrote a long and carefully reasoned letter to my father explaining this decision and what I foresaw as the post war development of the air transport industry, much of which looks remarkably prescient in the light of what has actually happened. I wrote this near to the end of the war and although it reached home I never received the reply. It was returned to my father stamped with what may have been the understatement of the year:

Returned by the Swiss Post Office who were unable to forward it to Germany because of the interruption of communications.

Anyway, recognising that I was determined, my father helped to get me an interview with the selection board for BOAC, the predecessor of British Airways. It took place in the offices of a distinguished firm of City stockbrokers and I was duly selected, but very soon came the catch. The conversion of RAF aircrew to civil flying was all being done by the RAF, and oh hell, I was now a civilian. Never mind, I comforted myself, surely it should be easy enough to get back temporarily into the service, so off I went to the Air Ministry where I had arranged an interview with a Penguin. Alas! I had not bargained with bureaucracy and the interviewer turned out to be a Penguin amongst Penguins. To my dismay he said no. There was no procedure to permit such a thing and anyway:

"What makes you think, Mr Morison, that trouble should be taken and public money spent just to serve your personal convenience?"

Perhaps, I suggested, after five years a grateful country might just—? But the Penguin said no, absolutely *NO*.

You bastard, I thought, and went away to become an accountant.

ENVOI

Auschwitz, Belsen, Dachau, Ravensbrück. Now that we know the horrors, our own little troubles have faded into insignificance.

Appendix A

SOME EXTRACTS FROM THE GENEVA CONVENTION OF 27 JULY, 1929, RELATIVE TO THE TREATMENT OF PRISONERS OF WAR.

PART I: GENERAL PROVISIONS

ARTICLE 1

The present Convention shall apply without prejudice to the stipulations of Part VII:—

(1) to all persons referred to in Articles 1,2 and 3 of the Regulations annexed to The Hague Convention of 18th October, 1907, concerning the Laws and Customs of War on Land, who are captured by the enemy.

(2) to all persons belonging to the armed forces of belligerents who are captured by the enemy in the course of operations of maritime or aerial war, subject to such exceptions (derogations) as the exceptions of such capture render inevitable. Nevertheless these exceptions shall not infringe the fundamental principles of the present Convention; they shall cease from the moment when the captured persons have reached a prisoner-of-war camp.

ARTICLE 2

Prisoners of war are in the power of the hostile Government, but not of the individuals or formation which captured them.

They shall at all times be humanely treated and protected, particularly against acts of violence, from insults and from public curiosity.

Measures of reprisal against them are fobidden.

Provided you were not a Jew or a Slav!

ARTICLE 3

Prisoners-of-war are entitled to respect for their persons and honour. Women shall be treated with all consideration due to their sex.

Prisoners shall retain their full civil capacity.

ARTICLE 4

The detaining Power is required to provide for the maintenance of prisoners of war in its charge.

Differences of treatment between prisoners are permissible only if such differences are based on military rank, the state of physical and mental health, the professional abilities, or the sex of those who benefit from them.

PART II: CAPTURE

ARTICLE 5

Every prisoner of war is required to declare, if he is interrogated on the subject, his true names and rank, or his regimental number.

If he infringes this rule, he exposes himself to a restriction of the privileges accorded to prisoners of his category.

No pressure shall be exerted on prisoners to obtain information regarding the situation in their armed forces or their country.

Prisoners who refuse to reply may not be threatened, insulted, or exposed to unpleasantness or disadvantages of any kind whatsoever.

Well, we were exposed to a few unpleasantnesses and disadvantages at Dulag.

ARTICLE 6

All personal effects and articles in personal use—except arms, horses, military equipment and military papers—shall remain in the possession of prisoners of war, as well as their helmets and gas-masks.

Sums of money carried by prisoners may only be taken from them on the order of an officer and after the amount has been recorded. A receipt shall be given for them. Sums thus impounded shall be placed to the account of each prisoner.

Their identity tokens, badges of rank, decorations and articles of clothing may not be taken from prisoners.

ARTICLE 11

The food ration of prisoners of war shall be equivalant in quantity and quality to that of the depot troops.

Prisoners shall also be afforded the means of preparing for themselves such additional articles of food as they may possess.

Sufficient drinking water shall be supplied to them. The use of tobacco shall be authorised.

Prisoners may be employed in the kitchens.

All collective disciplinary measures affecting food are prohibited.

German depot troops must have gone hungry unless they got Red Cross parcels!

ARTICLE 23

Subject to any special arrangements made between the belligerent Powers, and particularly those contemplated in Article 24, officers and persons of equivalent status who are prisoners of war shall receive from the detaining Power the same pay as officers of corresponding rank in the army of that Power, provided, however, that such pay does not exceed that to which they are entitled in the armed forces of the country in whose services they have been. This pay shall be paid to them in full, once a month if possible, and no deduction therefrom shall be made for expenditure devolving upon the detaining Power, even if such expenditure is incurred on their behalf.

An agreement between the belligerents shall prescribe the rate of exchange applicable to this payment; in default of such agreement, the rate of exchange adopted shall be that in force at the moment of the commencement of hostilities.

All advances made to prisoners of war by way of pay shall be reimbursed, at the end of hostilities, by the Power in whose services they were.

They would never have paid us in real money, so we got Lagermarks.

ARTICLE 50

Escaped prisoners of war who are re-captured before they have been able to rejoin their own armed forces or leave the territory occupied by the armed forces which captured them shall be liable only to disciplinary punishment.

ARTICLE 51

Attempted escape, even if it is not a first offence, shall not be considered as an aggravation of the offence in the event of the prisoner of war being brought before the courts for crimes or offences against persons or property committed in the course of such attempt.

After an attempted or successful escape, the comrades of the escaped person who aided the escape shall incur only disciplinary punishment therefor.

ARTICLE 52

Belligerents shall ensure that the competent authorities exercise the greatest leniency in considering the question whether an offence committed by a prisoner of war should be punished by disciplinary or by judicial measures.

This provision shall be observed in particular in appraising facts in connection with escape or attempted escape.

A prisoner shall not be punished more than once for the same act or on the same charge.

ARTICLE 54

Imprisonment is the most severe disciplinary puishment which may be inflicted on prisoners of war.

The duration of any single punishment shall not exceed thirty days.

This maximum of thirty days shall, moreover, not be exeeded in the event of there being several acts for which the prisoner is answerable to.

Articles 50 and 54 were the rules on which all escaping was based.

Appendix B

'THE LADIES' by Rudyard Kipling

I've taken my fun where I've found it;
I've rogued and I've ranged in my time;
I've had my pickin' o' sweethearts,
An' four o' the lot was prime.
One was an' 'arf caste widow,
One was a woman at Prome,
One was the wife of a *jemadar-sais*,
An' one is a girl at home.

Now I aren't no 'and with the ladies,
For takin' 'em all along,
You never can tell till you've tried 'em,
An' then you are like to be wrong.
There's times when you think that you mightn't;
There's times when you'll know that you might;
But the things that you'll learn from the yellow an' brown,
They'll 'elp you a lot with the white.

I was a young 'un at 'Oogli,
Shy as a girl to begin;
Aggie de Castrer she taught me,
An' Aggie was clever as sin;
Older than me, but my first 'un—
More like a mother she were—
Showed me the way to promotion an' pay,
An' I learned about women from 'er.

Then I was ordered to Burma,
Actin' in charge of bazaar,
An' I got me a tiddy live 'eathen
Through buyin' supplies from 'er pa.
Funny an' yellow an' faithful—
Doll in a tea cup she were—
But we lived on the square, like a true married pair,
An' I learned about women from 'er!

Then we was shifted to Neemuch
(Or I might ha' been keepin' 'er now),
An' I took with a shiny she-devil,
The wife of a nigger at Mhow;
Taught me the gipsey folk's *bolee*;
Kind o' volcano she were,
For she knifed me one night 'cause I wished she were white,
An' I learned about women from 'er!

Then I come 'ome in a trooper,
'Long of a kid of sixteen—
Girl from a convent at Meerut,
The straightest I ever 'ave seen.
Love at first sight were 'er trouble,
She didn't know what it were;
An' I wouldn't do such, 'cause I liked 'er to much,
But—I learned about women from 'er.

I've taken my fun where I found it,
An' now I must pay for my fun,
For the more you've known of the others
The less will you settle to one;
An' the end of it's sittin' and thinkin',
An' dreamin Hell-fires to see;
So be warned by my lot (which I know you will not),
An' learn about women from me!

What did the Colonel's Lady think?
Nobody never knew.
Somebody asked the Sergeant's wife,
An' she told 'em true!
They're like as a row of pins—
For the Colonel's lady and Judy O'Grady
Are sisters under their skins.

Appendix C

Bill Goldfinch's calculations for launching the Colditz Glider:

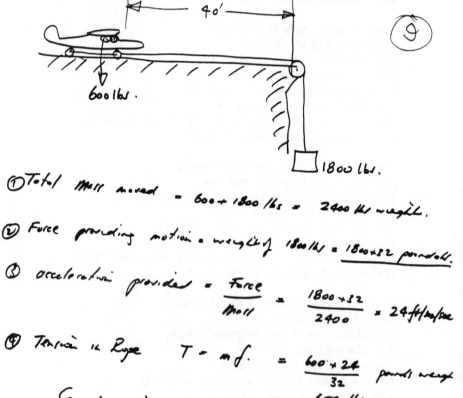

① Total mass moved = 600 + 1800 lbs = 2400 lbs weight.

② Force providing motion = weight of 1800 lbs = 1800×32 poundals.

③ acceleration provided = $\dfrac{Force}{Mass}$ = $\dfrac{1800 \times 32}{2400}$ = 24 ft/sec/sec

④ Tension in Rope   T = m.f. = $\dfrac{600 \times 24}{32}$ poundals weight

                                        = 450 lbs.

⑤ Time in seconds $(s = ut + \frac{1}{2}ft^2)$ = $\sqrt{\dfrac{40 \times 2}{24}}$ = 1·84 secs.

⑥ Velocity at end of run = 1·84 × 24 = 44 ft/sec
                                                    = 30 mph.

1800 lbs reduced by rolling resistance
                    + air drag.
             Velocity make this up.

Index

Index

If you have enjoyed this book, you may wish to know about other prisoner-of-war titles available from Sentinel Publishing:

MOONLESS NIGHT by B. A. James
'Jimmy' James, shot down and captured in June 1940, made a number of abortive escape attempts from Stalag Lufts I and III before taking part in the 'Great Escape' of March 1944. One of the seventy-six who got clear of the camp, he was also among the twenty-six spared the Gestapo bullet. Instead, he was sent to the concentration camp at Sachsenhausen—from which he also escaped.
'...a superb, a humbling book... The author is a modest man but, in spite of himself, his courage and his compassion—nobility is not too strong a word—pervade this remarkable book.'   *The Kriegie*

NO FLIGHT FROM THE CAGE by Calton Younger
Cal Younger's memoir is a monument to the legendary courage of Allied NCO aircrew in Stalag Lufts III and VI, and Stalag 357 at Thorn and Fallingbostel, as well as a moving tribute to Warrant Officer 'Dixie' Deans, the senior NCO to whom so many survivors owe their lives.
'*No Flight from the Cage* not only throws light on a curious and almost completely self-contained culture, the culture of the prison camp in war-time, it is also an adventure in the exploration of the human spirit whose total effect is both sobering and uplifting.'
General Sir John Hackett

FORCED MARCH TO FREEDOM by Robert Buckham
A pre-war graphic artist, Canadian pilot Robert Buckham recorded his impressions of Stalag Luft III in more than a hundred drawings and paintings. When the camp was evacuated in January 1945 they went with him, rolled up inside a tube made from tins soldered end-to-end. During the subsequent forced marches he kept a detailed diary and continued with his on-the-spot drawings. They were published in Canada as *Forced March to Freedom*, which received wide acclaim in two editions. This edition has been vastly expanded by the author, and includes a new chapter on his experiences in North Compound—where he forged documents for the 'Great Escape'—and a selection of his paintings.

BROKEN WINGS by Charles Rollings
The full story of Allied aircrew prisoners-of-war in Germany from September 1939 to May 1942. Packed with information made public for the first time, plus a lavish selection of photographs and drawings, it covers the period when aircrew POWs were dispersed throughout a number of camps in Germany prior to the opening of 'Göring's luxury camp', Stalag Luft III. From these camps they made hundreds of daring escapes, chalking up five home runs. *Broken Wings* is the first volume in the author's long-awaited four-volume history of Stalag Luft III.   *Available May 1995*

The following are in preparation:

LUFTGANGSTERS AT LARGE by Charles Rolling

The second volume in the author's history of Stalag Luft III, *Luftgangsters at Large* covers East and Centre compounds from April 1942 to April 1943; Oflag VIB, Warburg, from May 1942 to September 1942; and Oflag XXIB, Schubin, from September 1942 to April 1943. It climaxes in the mass escape from Schubin in March 1943 and the initial planning of the ill-fated 'Great Escape' from Stalag Luft III.   *Illustrated*

ITALIAN IMBROGLIO by Charles Rollings

This third volume in the history of Stalag Luft III follows the experiences of Allied aircrew prisoners-of-war who reached Sagan from Italy following the Armistice in September 1943. It also opens out the subject by telling the hitherto undisclosed story those who escaped from Italian prison camps and transport and either joined the partisans or sought shelter with the famous Rome Escape Line.

Illustrated

ICARUS BOUND by Charles Rollings

Volume Four of the Stalag Luft III story covers the period from April 1943 to the evacuation and liberation of the prisoners in 1945. The saga reaches repeated climaxes with the successful 'Wooden horse' escape in October 1943, the tragic 'Great Escape' in March 1944, and the rigours of the forced marches to Luckenwalde, Tarmstedt, Nuremburg and Moosburg in January 1945, followed by eventual liberation against the background of a nation in ruins.   *Illustrated*

For more information, please write to:
Sentinel Publishing, Carlton Lodge, 38 St. Ann's Road, London N15 6DU.
Tel.: 0181 800 0381.